Scope charity.
Leatherhead.
£1.75

LIFE IN THE TWENTIES AND THIRTIES

JOURNEYS INTO THE PAST

LIFE IN THE TWENTIES AND THIRTIES

Reader's Digest

Published by

THE READER'S DIGEST ASSOCIATION LIMITED

London   New York   Sydney
Montreal   Cape Town

SECRETS A British weekly magazine, which cost twopence in 1933.

BANK HOLIDAY New York State ordered banks to close, August, 1931. Depositors crowd the closed doors of the Union Bank, New York City.

LIFE IN THE TWENTIES AND THIRTIES
Edited and designed by Toucan Books Limited
Sole author: James Cochrane

First edition copyright © 1995
The Reader's Digest Association Limited,
Berkeley Square House, Berkeley Square, London W1X 6AB

Copyright © 1995
Reader's Digest Association Far East Limited
Philippines copyright © 1995
Reader's Digest Association Far East Limited

Printing and binding:
Printer Industria Gráfica S.A., Barcelona
Separations: Typongraph, Verona, Italy
Paper: Les Papeteries de Condat, Neuilly, France

ISBN 0 276 42127 2

Front cover (clockwise from top left): American couple dancing the Charleston; American face powder; Florida bathing beauties; British election poster; board game of the 1930s; cod-liver oil, Bovril and Fruit Salts; ticket to the Savoy Ballroom.

Back cover: Bonnie and Clyde; box of popcorn; poster for Sandeman port; Astor Theater on Times Square, New York; the Lincoln, an American car of the 1930s; a selection of comics from the 1930s.

Page 1: London street scene, from a London, Midland and Scottish railway poster, 1927.

Pages 2-3: Opening night of the movie *Grand Hotel* at the Astor Theater on Times Square, New York, 1932.

CONTENTS

RADIO DAYS
An Ekco wireless,
designed by
J.K. White, 1932.

CAMERA GIRL
The 'Kodak' girl,
in the mid 1930s.

OCEAN LINER The *Queen Mary*
in Southampton docks, 1934.

TRANSPORTS OF DELIGHT The Vickers-Vimy biplane
(above) lands in a bog at Clifden, Ireland, after the first
nonstop Atlantic air crossing by Alcock and Brown, 1919.
A page of motoring cut-outs (top) for children from a
Swedish family journal, 1927.

SCREEN IDOLS
Greta Garbo and
John Barrymore
star in the hit,
Grand Hotel, 1932.

THE LONG WEEKEND

In the years between the wars people moved from almost hysterical gaiety

to anxiety and despair, from the bright hopes of a better world to the miseries of

the Depression. But most people's standard of living was steadily improving.

T HE First and Second World Wars were great historical divides which changed the shape of the world for ever. The interval between the wars lasted just over 20 years – such a short time in the history of the world, and even in the lifetimes of those who lived through it, that Robert Graves and Alan Hodge, in their book about the period, called it *The Long Weekend*. Yet it was also an era of rapid and unprecedented change which dramatically altered the everyday lives of ordinary people.

An observer in January 1919, in a European city that had not been in the war zone, would have noticed at first very little that differed from January 1914. The buildings might have looked a little shabbier, and the atmosphere less cheerful; there would have been fewer young men around, and many of these might have lost a limb or possessed a strange, haunted look in their eyes and a nervous, jumpy manner – the effects of what had become known as 'shell shock'. But nearly all the buildings around dated from the 19th century or earlier. Although the streets were full of motor cars – particularly in the United States – there was still horse-drawn traffic in the streets. And planes, which had become a familiar sight in the war years, were not yet imagined as a form of commercial transport. There was electric street lighting, but most homes were still lit by gas or oil lamps. There were many cinemas, but they were small and showed only black-and-white silent films. At home wind-up gramophones were common, but there were no wireless sets and telephones were relatively rare, to be found mainly in offices. Most homes still had a Victorian clutter of heavy furniture, antimacassars, knick-knacks, heavily curtained windows, wood-burning stoves or coal fires. Older people still dressed much as they had in the early 1900s: men were still wearing homburg hats, beards, stiff collars and spats, and women still wore the fashions of Queen Victoria's last years.

The same observer, returning in January 1939, would have found the scene transformed. On the edge of the city there were modern, functional factory buildings and sprawling suburbs along roads built for motor transport. In the city itself there were smart office buildings and department stores, impressively palatial cinemas showing films in colour, modernistic apartment buildings and blocks of workers' flats. Only in the country could scenery that was not altered almost out of recognition be found.

The streets were crammed with closed motor cars, there were far fewer horse-drawn carts and the airliners passing overhead attracted little attention. Home interiors were less heavily furnished, airier and brighter. Most had electric lighting, and many also had electric fires. Nearly all had a wireless set, and many a telephone; a few had a refrigerator and a tiny minority even possessed a television set. People's clothes had also changed in a remarkable way. Most

AFTERMATH OF WAR German invalids from the First World War parade in the Kurfürstendamm, May 1919. The banner with the drawing of the beggar reads: 'This is the thanks of the Fatherland.'

FATHER THAMES An RAF plane, not unlike those of the First World War, flies over London, 1926. The south bank is still largely an industrial area and the new Waterloo Bridge, designed by Sir Giles Gilbert Scott, has not yet been built.

were ready-made and inexpensive rather than elaborately stitched by tailors and seamstresses, and working-class people in particular could afford to buy cheaper, much smarter clothes than was possible 20 years before. Even the character of popular music had changed dramatically in those 20 years, from the cheerful rhythms of ragtime and jazz-based dance music in 1919 to the very different sound of 1930s' swing and the smooth crooning of Bing Crosby and a young Frank Sinatra.

The imaginary observer of January 1919, might have noticed little change in the appearances of everyday life a few months after the First World War, but much had changed in people's minds. The survivors were mourning 9 million dead; millions more were physically or mentally damaged. The young men who had fought in the war returned less willing to submit to old injustices and old habits of deference to their 'betters'. Young women who had enjoyed good wages and lively companionship as war workers were less ready to accept that their only role in life was as wives and mothers or domestic servants. Everyone was aware that the old monarchies of Russia, Germany and Austria, which had looked as though they would last for eternity, had collapsed. They were aware, too, that a revolution in Russia in 1917 had turned into a bloody civil war, followed by a devastating famine in which millions were dying.

POSTWAR GERMANY

The Germans returned in 1918 to a country devastated by defeat and the harsh terms imposed on it by the Armistice and the Treaty of Versailles. The Allies had seized large numbers of Germany's transport lorries and railway goods trucks, so that the distribution of food and other vital supplies became next to impossible. In the months following the peace many thousands were reduced to near starvation. Many could be seen on the streets selling possessions in exchange for food; most were shabbily dressed, many in rags. Returning soldiers, still wearing their army uniforms, saw no hope of finding civilian employment. But before long, many of them found themselves being rearmed by the new socialist government in order to suppress a Communist revolution; others listened to the nationalist street orators, among them the young ex-soldier Adolf Hitler, who were calling for revenge, the restoration of German pride, and the destruction of the traitors who had betrayed her in 1918.

Germans felt deeply humiliated. Their country had lost a large part of its former territory; its foreign assets and its merchant fleet had been seized, and the sum of 269 thousand million gold marks had been

THE AMERICAN CENTURY New York bustled at night as well as during the day in the mid 1930s. George Gershwin (1898-1937), master of American popular music (left).

HARD TIMES South Dakota, 1936. Farmers, forced on relief by drought, are given government work mining gravel.

demanded by the Allies in reparations. This enormous sum of money was never paid in full. But the efforts to pay it were a terrible burden on the German people. The new German democratic government started to rebuild houses and factories with great speed and energy, but it had to print money to pay for the rebuilding, creating inflation for the future. The new government introduced some of the most advanced social welfare in the world, including unemployment pay, health insurance and subsidised public housing. Thousands of Germans moved from 19th-century industrial slums into bright modern flats with electric lighting and fitted kitchens; others left their villages to find work in modern factories. But as the economy deteriorated the government found it increasingly difficult to fulfil the promise of the early postwar years.

Weimar Berlin became a centre of social experiment, of sexual permissiveness and of avant-garde art; it was the city of satirical or erotic cabaret, of open homosexuality, where a young Marlene Dietrich dressed in men's clothes and the British writer Christopher Isherwood witnessed scenes of decadence that would one day be portrayed in the musical *Cabaret*. But all this stood in bleak contrast to the picture of political breakdown and social deprivation in the country as a whole. Many Germans loathed the permissiveness of Weimar Berlin; some probably foresaw that before long there would be a reaction.

In 1922-3 the Germans endured the nightmare of hyperinflation. So fast did prices rise that workers had to be paid several times a day; by evening a loaf of bread might cost what a house had cost in the morning. Visitors from abroad, with sterling or dollars in their wallets, could live like royalty on next

to nothing; those who were rich enough to speculate made fortunes. By 1924 the German currency had been stabilised, but the savings of millions of middle-class people had been made worthless – a source of resentment that the National Socialists were to feed on.

AMERICAN PROSPERITY

Americans, by contrast, returned to a country which had prospered greatly in the war – it now held most of the world's gold – and continued to prosper for ten years afterwards. Visitors marvelled not only at the magical new townscape created by the skyscrapers of New York and Chicago, then unique in the world, but also at the wealth of ordinary people. During the 1928 election campaign the Republicans promised 'a chicken in every pot and two cars in every garage', and that promise, unimaginable in Europe, seemed about to be realised across the Atlantic.

America came to symbolise everything that was bright and 'modern' and hopeful for the future of mankind. American manners had an uninhibited ease and freedom that young people everywhere strived to emulate. American music and dance styles were all the rage, as were American cocktails

DECADENT BERLIN
A cult magazine published in Germany in 1933. The cover depicts Berlin as a 'modern Babylon'.

based on gin, a drink previously thought to be very lower-class. Under American influence otherwise respectable young women were wearing lipstick and rouge and even dyeing their eyelashes. American films already dominated the world entertainment industry. Apparently free from Victorian feelings of guilt about worldly pleasures, Americans were throwing themselves into all the delights of the new age of leisure that was dawning.

Rich Americans, their pockets full of strong dollars, invaded debt-ridden Europe to buy castles, art treasures and antiques. The ancient manor houses of Great Lodge in Essex and Agecroft Hall in Lancashire were sent, stone by stone, to the United States, along with one of Britain's most famous paintings, the *Blue Boy* by Gainsborough, formerly owned by the Duke of Westminster. Even relatively poor Americans such as Ernest Hemingway and Scott Fitzgerald found they could live well in Paris or Berlin for a few dollars a week.

Somewhere between the two extremes represented by German poverty and North American prosperity came the other countries of Western Europe. France, sadly weakened by her efforts in the war and less industrialised than Britain and Germany, was slower to modernise; there was social unrest in her industrial cities that sometimes erupted into violent riots and demonstrations, but life in her smaller towns and villages went on much as it had in the 19th century; the building boom did not really start in France until after the Second World War. On the one hand, France was a world leader in motor-car design and manufacture; on the other, large parts of the country were still without electricity, and the millions of French peasants would not have noticed much change in their everyday lives from their grandparents' days.

BRITAIN'S PROBLEMS

The British muddled along, now a debtor rather than a creditor nation, and one that had lost a large share of her world trade to countries such as America and Japan. Britain suffered serious unemployment even in the relatively prosperous 1920s and was not free of

---

EYEWITNESS

'HE HAD LOOKED VERY LONGINGLY AT THE APPLES'

IN 1922 WHILE travelling in Europe, Ernest Hemingway and his wife crossed from France into Germany. The fever of hyperinflation in Germany had begun, though it was not yet at its worst.

❦ There were no marks to be had in Strasbourg, the mounting exchange had cleaned the bankers out days ago, so we changed some French money in the railway station at Kehl. For 10 francs I received 670 marks. Ten francs amounted to about 90 cents in Canadian money. That 90 cents lasted Mrs Hemingway and me for a day of heavy spending and at the end of the day we had 120 marks left!

Our first purchase was from a fruit stand beside the main street of Kehl where an old woman was selling apples, peaches and plums. We picked out five very good-looking apples and gave the old woman a 50 mark note. She gave us back 38 marks in change. A very nice-looking, white-bearded old gentleman saw us buy the apples and raised his hat.

"Pardon me, sir," he said, rather timidly, in German, "how much were the apples?"

I counted the change and told him 12 marks. He smiled and shook his head.

"I can't pay, it is too much."

He went up the street walking very much as white-bearded old gentlemen of the old regime walk in all countries, but he had looked very longingly at the apples. I wish I had offered him some. Twelve marks, on that day, amounted to a little under 2 cents.

The old man, whose life's savings were probably, as most of the non-profiteer classes are, invested in German prewar and war bonds, could not afford a 12 mark expenditure. He is a type of the people whose incomes do not increase with the falling purchasing power of the mark and the krone. . . .

Kehl's best hotel, which is a very well turned-out place, served a five course table d'hôte meal for 120 marks, which amounts to 15 cents in our money. The same meal could not be duplicated in Strasbourg, three miles away, for a dollar. ❦

ROOTS OF NAZISM Unemployed people in Germany queue for newspapers in the hope of finding advertisements offering some form of work in the early 1930s. Adolf Hitler (right), photographed in 1923, the year of the failed Nazi putsch.

social conflict, which came to a head in the General Strike of 1926. For nine days in May that year, with armed troops in the streets and 300 000 mainly middle-class volunteers keeping essential services going, it looked to some observers as if class antagonism was going to ignite into revolution. Somehow, however, the nation, though weaker than in its Victorian heyday, held together. Those who had jobs found themselves with spare money, and the growing consumer society provided a wider choice of things to buy. Their shorter working hours meant they could enjoy weekends and take annual holidays. Overall, the British people were fitter, healthier and better fed than they had ever been before.

A GERMAN REVOLUTION National Socialist posters such as this one promised Germans 'Work, Freedom and Bread'.

These halcyon days came to an abrupt end with the Wall Street Crash of 1929 which was the watershed of the period. The 'Roaring Twenties' and 'The Jazz Age', in which a relatively small but highly visible number of people had danced their nights away with frantic, brittle gaiety, and a rather larger number enjoyed increasing prosperity, seemed to be over, at least temporarily. People hoped for better times to come. In the USA in the late 1920s there had been a fever of speculation in which, it seemed, the whole nation had joined. The New York stock market went up and up; tens of thousands of people borrowed money to buy shares that looked as if they were going to climb in value for ever. But the bubble was soon to burst. Joseph Kennedy, father of the US president, decided to sell his shares, he later claimed, after he heard a shoeshine boy offering investment advice outside

11

EMPIRE HOPES Poster for the British Empire Exhibition at Wembley, 1925, when Britain still had an Empire.

the Stock Exchange, and thus saved his fortune. He was one of the lucky ones. The market plunged in October 1929. Ruined millionaires really did jump out of skyscraper windows on Wall Street, and millions of ordinary Americans lost everything they had. The market did eventually recover, and some of those who held on or bought after the Crash were able to accumulate new fortunes. But the damage had been done. As American investment dried up and the collapse of confidence spread to banks and stock exchanges elsewhere, the effects were felt all around the world.

THE DEPRESSION

After the Great Crash came the Great Depression, which cast tens of millions out of work around the world and millions of others into misery and despair. Farmers found that the prices they were getting for the food they produced were lower than the cost of producing it. Industrial firms with falling order books had to shed their labour. Bewildered men everywhere found themselves with no work to go to; some of them were to walk hundreds of miles following the merest rumour of a job. Shopkeepers became destitute when the communities they served could no longer afford to buy from them. Former professional men sold matches in the street or joined the soup kitchen queues.

The tidal wave that flowed from the Crash of 1929 reached as far as Australia, where more than 25 per cent of workers lost their employment, and in the early 1930s emigration from the country actually exceeded immigration. Everywhere in the world was

affected, but the effects were uneven. Germany was very badly hit; the French, so many of whom still lived close to the land and to local markets, were among those who could reduce their expectations and continue to eat and drink well, even if they could no longer afford the 'luxury' of consumer durables.

In 1932 the United States, facing total economic and social collapse, adopted a democratic solution by voting in Franklin Roosevelt as President. His 'New Deal' – a programme of job creation, public works and welfare legislation – changed the mood of the country almost overnight by giving people hope. Things began to improve, but high unemployment continued until America started armaments manufacturing towards the end of the 1930s as a new war loomed.

In 1933 Germany elected Hitler and the National Socialists to power. The job-creation programmes of the Nazis – mainly of public works as in the United States but also of almost immediate rearmament – reduced unemployment radically. Many Germans felt a growing sense of hope, dignity and national pride.

From the late 1920s on, there was a lot of war news on the wireless. In 1935 Mussolini's Italy invaded Abyssinia; and in 1936 Republicans and Nationalists fought the Spanish Civil War. The Russians supplied arms to the Republicans, and Italy and Germany sent arms to the Nationalists. But before the civil war was over, it was becoming clear in Europe that war with Hitler was inevitable. With the memories of the First World War still fresh in their minds, people contemplated the possibility of another war with horror.

FAMILY LIFE BETWEEN THE WARS

Families had become smaller. Sexual behaviour had

become looser, but official public morality was still strict.

Women were enjoying more freedom, and men and women

were spending more time together than ever before.

Home-life became more important and children were cherished.

But poverty still blighted the lives of many families.

MEN AND WOMEN

Men and women were beginning to have more romantic expectations about marriage,

and were sometimes disappointed. Meanwhile, the 'flappers' were determined to

show that life before marriage could be fun.

I N 1918, in the capitals of the victorious Allies, huge crowds had celebrated the armistice amid scenes of hysterical jubilation. Complete strangers were seen embracing in doorways. However, not very many active servicemen were present at these celebrations, since most of them were still in Europe and the Middle East, awaiting demobilisation. Many of those who have left memoirs of the time record their reaction to the end of the war as one of dazed relief. When eventually they returned to their homes, few of these young men (even those who had escaped wounding or the insidious effects of 'shell shock') were left unchanged by the experience of war. Farmboys from the United States and Canada, South Africa, Australia and New Zealand, who had never travelled far from their homes before taking ship for France or Egypt, went back feeling restless, having glimpsed another world – 'How're you gonna keep them down on the farm, now that they've seen Paree?' – a popular song of the time asked.

Young Britishers and Frenchmen and Germans might not have travelled so many miles, but their mental horizons had also expanded, and they had shed their old habits of deference to their former masters. The American Scott Fitzgerald wrote that no war could ever be fought again the way the First World War had been fought, for men would no longer be found obedient enough to march towards the enemy's barbed wire and machine guns. Time and time again veterans reported their reluctance to talk, especially to civilians, about what they had seen and done, but the

changed mental attitudes of millions of returning servicemen must surely have had something to do with the frenetic, sometimes violent, character of the postwar years (and its dramatic social changes).

The generation of young men and women who survived the First World War tended to reject the moral certainties that had led to that tragic folly – or at least failed to prevent it – and with them the stricter social conventions. Social attitudes generally were more relaxed. Young people now had far more opportunities to meet unchaperoned, in the workplace, at parties, and in the wide range of places such as dance halls, clubs or skating rinks where they spent their leisure time. Because of the terrible loss of life in the war there were, of course, many fewer men than women in their late twenties and thirties in the European countries that had taken part in it, especially among the upper classes, which had suffered a higher percentage of fatalities. Though this was offset to some extent for the population as a whole by a reduction in the rate of male emigration, there were many women born in the generation of the 1890s who never married because the men who might have become their husbands were dead. In Germany alone the surplus of women over men was 1 million.

Young women too had changed. American women had long enjoyed far less social restraint than European women. This was attributed to the fact that in the War of Independence, and again in the Civil War, they had grown used to carrying on in the absence of their menfolk. In the same

WAR'S END An American soldier, with souvenir flags, about to embark at St Nazaire in France for the voyage home at the end of the First World War.

Let's Dance Social barriers came down. Men and women of all classes at the Bal Musette, Paris, in the early 1920s.

way the demand for women workers during the First World War went some way towards freeing at least the younger generation of British and European women.

FLAPPERS

The more liberated young women of the 1920s were known as 'flappers', particularly if they had slim figures. In Germany, where the cult of this kind of boyish shape had first become fashionable, the flapper was known as a *backfisch*. In France, where women's bodies did not typically conform with the desired tall, slim outline, the fashion came relatively late, but by the mid 1920s flappers could be seen in cities everywhere, from Berlin to San Francisco and from Montreal to Melbourne. Because of the rationing of sugar and butter during the war, and the increased popularity of swimming and of games like hockey and tennis, women had become slimmer.

EYEWITNESS

'A RATHER STUFFY VICTORIAN FAMILY'

❛ England is not the jewelled isle of Shakespeare's much-quoted passage, nor is it the inferno depicted by Dr Goebbels. More than either it resembles a family, a rather stuffy Victorian family, with not many black sheep in it but with all its cupboards bursting with skeletons. It has rich relations who have to be kow-towed to and poor relations who are horribly sat upon, and there is a deep conspiracy of silence about the source of the family income. It is a family in which . . . most of the power is in the hands of irresponsible uncles and bedridden aunts. Still, it is a family. It has a private language and common memories, and at the approach of an enemy it closes its ranks. A family with the wrong members in control – that, perhaps, is as near as one can come to describing England in a phrase. ❜

From *England Your England and Other Essays* **by George Orwell**

Apart from their new cylindrical shape, and the flimsy clothing that went with it, flappers were noted for behaviour that the more conservative elements in society, and especially the Church, found shocking. They danced very close to their partners and showed a great deal of leg when dancing the 'shimmy' or the Charleston. They were to be heard using the bad language that had become familiar during the war years. They frequented bars and public houses and smoked in public. (For a woman to smoke in a fashionable restaurant soon became acceptable, but it was regarded as very improper for her to do so when riding on a bus or on the street.) They were to be seen riding on the pillions – known as the 'flapper brackets' – of motorcycles. All in all, they were less submissive, more 'brazen' than women were traditionally supposed to be. Their brazenness, it was sometimes suggested, was something they had learned as flagsellers during the war and in the years just after, when there were flag days for one cause or another almost every week and

young women grew used to approaching men on the street. The flapper look was not merely a matter of fashion; it represented a feminine ideal of the postwar years. The American historian Frederick Allen observed, writing in 1931:

'. . . the quest of slenderness, the flattening of the breasts, the vogue of short skirts (even when short skirts still suggested the appearance of a little girl), the juvenile effect of the long waist – all were signs that, consciously or unconsciously, the women of this decade worshipped not merely youth, but unripened youth: they wanted to be – or thought men wanted them to be – men's casual and light-hearted companions; not broad-hipped mothers of the race, but irresponsible playmates . . . In effect, the woman of the Post-War Decade said to man: "You are tired and disillusioned, you do not want the cares of a family or the companionship of mature wisdom, you want exciting play, you want the thrills of sex without their fruition, and I will give them to you." And to herself she added, "But I will be free." '

SEX AND MORALITY

Private sexual morals were more relaxed than before, and more and more men and women had at least some sexual experience before marriage. Americans in particular worried about the loosening of morals since the war, especially among the young. Scott Fitzgerald's novel *This Side of Paradise*, published in 1920, shocked American parents with its revelations about 'petting parties'. He wrote: 'None of the Victorian mothers – and most of the mothers were Victorian – had any idea how casually their daughters were accustomed to be kissed.'

The change was attributed to the scantiness of young women's clothing and the closeness with which young men and women

STYLISH ERA An American flapper (above) poses by her roadster. Scott Fitzgerald (left), whose writing perfectly caught the spirit of the era.

AVIATOR Lindbergh and the *Spirit of St Louis* at Curtiss Field, Long Island, before the transatlantic flight.

AN AMERICAN HERO: CHARLES LINDBERGH

ON SATURDAY, MAY 21, 1927, traffic in and around Paris virtually came to a stop as a crowd estimated at half a million people struggled to reach Le Bourget airport.

They were there to witness the arrival of a young American airmail pilot called Charles Lindbergh who had just completed the first solo nonstop transatlantic flight from Roosevelt Field in New York, flying his monoplane *Spirit of St Louis* without a radio, and with no instruments other than a magnetic compass. On the evening before, at the Yankee Stadium in New York, 40 000 boxing fans had stood in bare-headed silence when the announcer asked them to pray for him. At 10.20 pm his plane touched down, to a welcome that could only be described as ecstatic. The Paris correspondent of the London *Daily Mail* reported:

'Thousands of people fought among themselves and struggled with burly policemen to get near Lindbergh and shake his hand. Women who had sworn to kiss him had their fur cloaks torn to shreds and emerged from the fray with their hats gone, their hair dishevelled and their dresses tattered and torn.'

Ten people were taken to hospital. The fabric of the plane was ripped to provide souvenirs, and Lindbergh himself had to be rescued by soldiers wielding rifle butts.

Overnight, the fair-haired, blue-eyed American from Little Falls, Minnesota, had become famous. Poems were written for him, children baptised with his name, and drinks named after him. On May 28, he flew to Brussels and on the following day to London's Croydon airport, to be greeted by a crowd even more frenzied than the one at Le Bourget.

He was received by King George V at Buckingham Palace and was a guest of the Prince of Wales. When eventually he returned to the United States, by ship this time, a crowd estimated at 4.5 million turned out to the ticker-tape parade in his honour up Broadway. He was literally worshipped. Huge material rewards and inducements to lend his name to advertising were offered to him, all of which he rejected. He met all the most prominent men of the day, and handled these encounters with striking charm, modesty and tact. He did not smoke or dance or drink anything but milk or water. He was compared with Joan of Arc, Lafayette, even Christ.

Lindbergh's fame – greater than that enjoyed by America's astronauts after their walk on the Moon – remains a mystery. Newspaper editors recognised that it was the biggest news story since the war, at a time when there were more newspapers and readers then than ever before or since. But newspaper coverage seems to have followed rather than stimulated the excitement that surrounded this first solo nonstop crossing of the Atlantic. It was as if people saw in the young pilot's achievement a symbol that touched something very deep within: a triumph over death, which itself had seemed triumphant less than ten years before; an angelic flight from a bright new world of hope to an old one worn out from its struggles.

The rest of Charles Lindbergh's life was tarnished by tragedy. In 1932 his baby son was murdered by kidnappers. In the 1930s, too, he opposed America's entry into the Second World War and was thought to have Nazi sympathies. His life in some ways epitomises the course that America took in the interwar years from being the hope of the world after the war to isolationism and despair in the depressed 1930s.

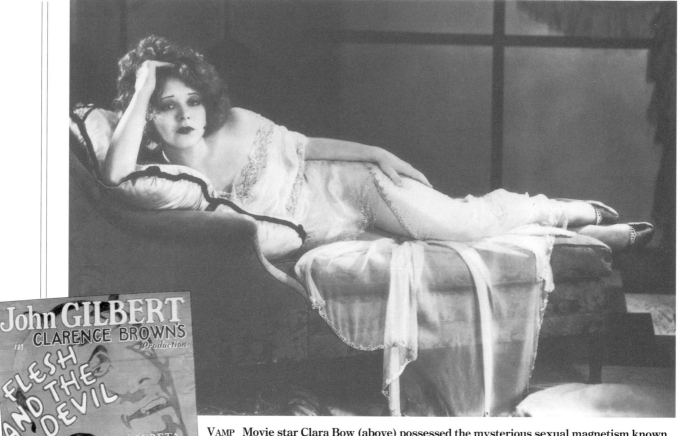

VAMP Movie star Clara Bow (above) possessed the mysterious sexual magnetism known as 'It', and movies, like the one advertised (left), reflected the new sexual freedom.

now danced – 'The men won't dance with you if you wear a corset', girls were quoted as saying. Prohibition, and the great increase in drinking – especially among women – that resulted from it, probably had something to do with it, along with the availability of the closed automobile (90 per cent of American cars were open in 1919; by 1927 more than 80 per cent were closed). Robert and Helen Lynd in their famous 1920s study of a typical American city, *Middletown*, wrote that boys and girls now thought nothing of jumping into a car and driving off to a dance in another town 20 miles (32 km) away, where they were strangers and could enjoy a freedom impossible among their neighbours. The closed car, they noted, was in effect a room protected from the weather, and could be moved at any time of day into a darkened side street or a country lane.

Then there were the confession magazines with articles such as: 'What I Told My Daughter the Night Before her Marriage' and 'Indolent Kisses'. And, of course, there were the movies. In the early 1920s, before the Hays Office began to impose censorship on the output of Hollywood, the producers promoted films promising 'beautiful jazz babies, champagne baths, midnight revels, petting parties in the purple dawn' or 'neckers, petters, white kisses, red kisses, pleasure-mad daughters, sensation-craving mothers . . . the truth – bold, naked, sensational'.

The America of the 1920s was probably, as in so many things, ahead of most of Europe in sexual matters but, in other countries too, sexual knowledge had greatly increased. This was partly through deliberate public education – which was especially encouraged in Weimar Germany – but also because young women were less isolated than before and could learn from the gossip of work companions. Family planning was practised more and more, encouraged by pioneers such as the British woman

HOOFERS Doing the Charleston, a dance that helped women to shed some restricting underwear. Wearing a corset made it impossible to achieve the abandon necessary for its performance.

Marie Stopes, whose book *Married Love* of 1918 was internationally influential. A British survey showed that whereas only 20 per cent of married women in mid-Victorian Britain attempted to limit their families, more than 70 per cent of those marrying between the wars did so. Condoms were selling in large numbers by the 1930s (the leading British manufacturer was selling 20 million a year) and reliable diaphragms were available. Older methods were used by the poorer classes. Pessaries were made at home from lard, margarine and flour, cocoa butter and quinine, and *coitus interruptus* was still a widely used method.

Official and public morality were still strict by today's standards. If women practised premarital sex it was not something to which they would publicly admit, and illegitimacy was deeply shameful. Books were strictly censored, particularly for sexual explicitness or any suggestion of female enjoyment of the sexual act; this is why James Joyce's *Ulysses* and D.H. Lawrence's *Lady Chatterley's Lover* were banned in Britain (*Ulysses* had to be cleared by a judge in the USA before it could be published). In America the Hays Office vetted all films from 1922 and, in the 1930s, the Catholic League of Decency also watched them closely to ensure that, for example, married couples used twin beds and were never seen sleeping together. Even film titles had to be squeaky clean: one called *Infidelity* had to be renamed *Fidelity*.

Discussion of sexual matters, for example in women's magazines, was still coy. Advertisements for maternity dresses referred to pregnancy in euphemisms such as 'that interesting condition' and promised to 'keep your secret'. The Roman Catholic Church condemned any form of birth control other than abstinence, and even the Anglican Bishop of Southwark in London could state that the breakup of a marriage was better than sexual intercourse for

FOOLISH THINGS A cigarette was *the* fashion accessory; members of the young generation on Long Island.

'THERE ARE JOBS FOR EVERYBODY EXCEPT THE DRUNKS'

IN A FAMOUS ESSAY on boys' comics, written in 1939, George Orwell compares them with the women's fiction magazines of the day, where characters inhabited an idealised world in which life's problems and setbacks are only temporary:

❛ The women's papers are aimed at an older public and are read for the most part by girls who are working for a living. Consequently they are on the surface much more realistic. It is taken for granted, for example, that nearly everyone has to live in a big town and work at a more or less dull job. Sex, so far from being taboo, is *the* subject. The short, complete stories, the special feature of these papers, are generally of the "came the dawn" type: the heroine narrowly escapes losing her "boy" to a designing rival, or the "boy" loses his job and has to postpone marriage, but presently gets a better job. The changeling fantasy (a girl brought up in a poor home is "really" the child of rich parents) is another favourite. Where sensationalism comes in, usually in the serials, it arises out of the more domestic type of crime, such as bigamy, forgery or sometimes murder; no Martians, death-rays or international anarchist gangs. These papers are at any rate aiming at credibility, and they have a link with real life in their correspondence columns, where genuine problems are being discussed. Ruby M. Ayres's column of advice in the *Oracle*, for instance, is extremely sensible and well-written. And yet the world of

PROPHET OF GLOOM George Orwell wrote about the failure of the British Establishment, but had no illusions about totalitarian Communism.

the *Oracle* and *Peg's Paper* is pure fantasy-world. It is the same fantasy all the time; pretending to be richer than you are. The impression that one carries away from almost all these papers is of a frightful, overwhelming "refinement". Ostensibly the characters are working-class people, but their habits, the interiors of their houses, their clothes, their outlook

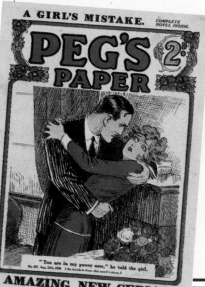

OFFICE AFFAIR A Fate Worse than Death is to befall the heroine – but rescue is imminent.

and, above all, their speech are entirely middle class. They are all living at several pounds a week above their income. And, needless to say, that is just the impression that is intended. The idea is to give the bored factory-girl or worn-out mother of five a dream-life in which she pictures herself – not actually as a duchess (that convention has gone out) but as, say, the wife of a bank manager. Not only is a five-to-six pound-a-week standard of living set up as the ideal, but it is tacitly assumed that that is how working-class people really *do* live. The major facts are simply not faced. It is admitted, for instance, that people sometimes lose their jobs; but then the dark clouds roll away and they get better jobs instead. No mention of unemployment as something permanent and inevitable, no mention of the dole, no mention of trade unionism. No suggestion anywhere that there can be anything wrong with the system as a *system*; there are only individual misfortunes, which are generally due to somebody's wickedness and can in any case be put right in the last chapter. Always the dark clouds roll away, the kind employer raises Alfred's wages; and there are jobs for everybody except the drunks. It is still the world of the *Wizard* and the *Gem*, except that there are orange blossoms instead of machine guns. ❜

HOLLYWOOD MODESTY Observing the proprieties, Merle Oberon and Melvyn Douglas in *That Uncertain Feeling* (above), and Claudette Colbert and Clark Gable in *It Happened One Night* (left), all demurely occupy twin beds.

'mere gratification'. Another Anglican bishop condemned contraception on the grounds that the French used it and had thereby reduced their national birthrate to such an extent that they were obliged to import foreign labour.

The British Home Secretary of the 1920s banned mixed bathing in London's Serpentine lake, and the London Underground banned an advertisement showing a woman in a backless evening dress.

Few authorities went as far as the town of Norphelt, Arkansas, which passed an ordinance in 1925, stating: *Section 1. Hereafter it shall be unlawful for any man and woman, male or female, to be guilty of committing the act of sexual intercourse between* *themselves at any place within the corporate limits of said town.* Citizens of Norphelt had to read on to Section 3 of the ordinance to find it qualified as follows: *Section 1 of this ordinance shall not apply to married persons as between themselves, and their husband and wife, unless of a grossly improper and lascivious nature.*

Among the exceptions to this public prudishness were Paris and Weimar Berlin, where there was virtually no censorship of books and where, for example, homosexuality was tolerated and gay and

---

LITERARY FIRSTS

Marguerite Radclyffe Hall's *The Well of Loneliness* (1928), the first novel in English to treat lesbianism in a mature way, was banned in the UK after an obscenity trial. Even 'straight' sex could not be discussed explicitly in public. In 1927, after the publication of Elinor Glyn's novel *It*, the book's title was used for years as a euphemism for sex appeal.

lesbian magazines were freely available for sale. After 1933 the Nazis, ironically, enforced a very strict public morality and imprisoned homosexuals and 'deviants'.

Abortion was still illegal almost everywhere. Only in Sweden was it legalised in 1938. Women resorted to self-inducement methods, using violent purgatives such as penny royal, slippery elm and ergot of rye, or even oxide of lead, or the traditional combination of gin, hot baths and violent exertion. The British writer Ted Willis describes his own mother's (unsuccessful) efforts to prevent his birth:

'She bought gin she could ill-afford and drank it neat. She carried the tin bath in from the back yard, filled it to near boiling with water and then lowered herself into it, scalding her flesh so painfully that she was in agony for days. She ran up and down stairs until she was exhausted. And when all this failed to check my progress, she procured some gunpowder –

enough to cover a sixpence – mixed it with a pat of margarine, and swallowed it. This was reckoned in those days to be almost infallible, but it succeeded only in making her violently ill.'

If these methods failed, women all too often resorted to backstreet abortionists, with tragic consequences for untold numbers of them. Illegal abortions were the other side of the coin of strict public morality. So was prostitution, which was still a major social problem, visible on the streets of all major cities. The poet Robert Graves, among others, observed that, faced with competition from increasing numbers of 'amateurs', professional prostitutes had become smarter in dress, healthier, and more tactful when approaching clients. In the Depression years especially, many women resorted to prostitution as an alternative to starvation. Among the 2 million Americans who were on the road looking for work in

ON THE STREET In Europe, prostitutes openly solicited in the years between the wars (above). The poster from Germany (left) offers the movie-goer glimpses of decadence.

ROMANCE Greta Garbo and John Barrymore smoulder in *Grand Hotel* (above) and romance permeates the usually prosaic pages of a women's magazine (right).

1932 there were hundreds of nomad prostitutes offering their services for as little as 10 cents. In Germany the Nazis, as part of their law-and-order drive, cleared the prostitutes from the streets. The French, on the other hand, had licensed and medically supervised brothels.

By the end of the 1920s much of the frantic excitement of the postwar sexual revolution had evaporated: there was less talk of the joys of unfettered Free Love and less debunking of traditional morality. In general, however, sexual relations between men and women were more equal, and freer of Victorian ignorance and guilt.

LOVE AND MARRIAGE

Nineteenth-century poets and novelists had celebrated romantic love. In practice, however, the Victorians had largely believed in considerations of 'suitability' as a basis for marriage. Were the couple compatible in temperament? Could the husband support the wife in the fashion to which she had been accustomed? Did the wife bring any fortune of her own to the partnership? Would she produce healthy children and be a prudent and thrifty housekeeper? If satisfactory answers could be provided to these questions, the Victorians believed love would grow.

In the 1920s and 30s considerations of this kind persisted in more traditional rural communities, and especially in the countries of the Mediterranean. The upper classes too still held the debutante balls of the 'Season' that were designed to introduce young women to a range of young men carefully vetted for their suitability.

Peasants and aristocrats still made arranged marriages but, for the urban young, the notion of love alone as a sound reason for marrying had become firmly established, and was reinforced by the popular songs of the period and by popular fiction, the cinema and women's magazines. It was as if the idea of romantic love, which had developed among a

---

DOOMED DREAMER

In 1922 Edith Thompson and her lover Freddy Bywaters were hanged for the murder of Edith's husband, Percy. Inspired by the plots of cheap novelettes, Edith had devised various schemes for killing her husband, but there was no evidence that she had attempted to carry any of them out. In the end Freddy stabbed Percy, and Edith was found guilty with him, more of immorality than murder.

HIGH SOCIETY A popular society wedding in London. Margaret Whigham marries American golfer Charles Sweeney.

'TO HAVE HIS DINNER READY ON TIME'

MARRIED WOMEN in the 1920s and 30s who worked had a double burden, and often a demanding schedule at home and at work, especially if they were as devoted as this German textile worker, who describes a typical day.

❛ At six o'clock my alarm goes off and thus begins my workday. Washing and dressing are my first jobs; as for grooming, there's not much to do in that regard because I have short hair. Then I put on water for coffee and get some bread and butter ready for my husband and me. With that I'm ready and it's also time to wake my husband because he has a half hour bike ride to his workplace. While he's getting dressed, I get his bicycle ready. I pump air in the tyres and fasten on his lunchbox. He drinks his coffee and soon he's on his way. I go to the front window and wave him goodbye. Now it's 7.45 am and I must quickly bring a little order to the place. I have only a small apartment, but it nonetheless takes some doing in order to make it look right. At 8.15 I also have to leave. I work in the coloured-pattern weaving section from 8.30 to 12.30 without stop. I eat my breakfast about 9. But I don't let my looms stop; they continue working, for when one works by contract, one has to keep going in order to earn something. At 12.30 it's time for lunch and I return home quickly. After eating, I clean the hall and stairs, and meanwhile it's 1.45 and time to go. Work then goes from 2 to 5 without stop. But when it's five, I go back to my little place with a happy heart. Then my husband soon returns, and I have always taken great pains to have his dinner ready on time. Then I wash the dishes and my husband reads me the newspaper. ❜

privileged aristocracy in the Middle Ages, had at last percolated down to the level of ordinary people. One reason for this was economic: freed by increasing prosperity from the struggle merely to survive, people developed higher expectations of life, including the idea that it could be more exciting.

Another reason was that many young women were working away from their homes. In life, as in romantic fiction, people were meeting and marrying partners unknown to their parents or their own communities – quite unheard-of just a few years before.

In traditional agricultural societies couples spent their wedding night together within the community; they might even be accompanied to the marriage bed by their neighbours and visited there by them in the small hours of the morning. Wedding celebrations in the village might last several days, and then the couple would put away their wedding clothes and resume their work within the community, their labours divided and defined by tradition. However, in the urban society of the 1920s and 30s, the young couple would change into going-away clothes after the wedding ceremony and then depart for their honeymoon. On their return, they might well move into a house or a flat far from where either had been brought up. They would probably have a wider circle of friends and acquaintances than their parents had known, and they might even communicate with them by telephone and visit them by car. On the one hand, they lived in a wider world; on the other, they lived, as a couple, in greater isolation than people in traditional communities. Increasingly, too, they saw themselves as consumers, as well as producers. In North America the average amount spent on themselves tripled between 1909 and 1930, with the most striking increases being for clothes, cosmetics and toiletries, furniture, household appliances, cars and recreation.

'LIFE'S NOT SO DUSTY' If this advertisement from the 1920s is to be believed, carpet-cleaning ensures married bliss.

An Evening at the Cinema

THEY WERE DREAM PALACES where, especially in the 1930s, people could escape from the dreary realities of life to a world of excitement, glamour and romance. Hollywood believed audiences did not want films that reflected real life, but would welcome spending a few hours watching films about exotic places or the lives of the idle rich. The new cinemas, with their soft seats, carpeting and bright, modernist decor, were much more comfortable than many people's homes. They had bars, tearooms and sold ice cream. Both the daytime and evening performances provided a main and second feature, newsreels, cartoons and a short documentary or comedy feature. All this and a magnificent theatre organ which would rise up to play during the intermissions.

PARENTS AND CHILDREN

With smaller families and greater leisure, parents could now devote more time to their children.

Relationships within the family were more relaxed, but children were

still expected to be obedient, both at home and at school.

THERE WAS a great change in the nature of marriage in the years following the First World War. People of all classes now regarded having only two children as the desirable norm: the average French couple produced fewer than two children throughout the interwar years, the German birthrate dropped to half its 1900 level – and figures were similar almost everywhere else in the Western world. Children were much more likely to survive infancy and, as child labour was becoming rarer, large families were no longer seen as having economic value, except in peasant communities. On the contrary, the cost of larger families was now seen as a burden. For the middle classes it meant, among other things, high school fees and expensive domestic help in the nursery. For the working class, a smaller family meant that wages could be spent on leisure activities and goods rather than on basics such as food and clothing.

There was yet another change. In traditional societies, men and women had spent much of their social lives apart, as they still do today in the small towns and villages of Mediterranean countries. Victorian gentlemen devoted many of their leisure hours to male society in their clubs, while their womenfolk stayed at home. Similarly, men of the urban working class had traditionally spent their few hours of leisure with other males in cafés, bars or pubs. Couples in the new urban society of the interwar years were spending more time with each other and with their children. One reason for this was simply that, with shorter working hours, they had more leisure to do so. Probably another was that more confident wives, themselves less burdened by work, demanded that they should. But, as far as working-class people were concerned, there was yet another reason: the cramped conditions in which so many of the urban working class had lived in previous decades

GOOD NEWS OR BAD? The late 1930s, and a young middle-class Berlin family listen to the news – with apprehension.

THIRTIES FAMILIES A society mother, father, child and nanny in London (above). Farther down the social scale, Oklahoma refugees in New Mexico (left).

meant that the home was at best a place in which to eat and sleep, but better and more spacious accommodation in the 1920s and 30s meant that it could now be a place in which to enjoy free time with the family. Men and women also went out together more: cinemas, bars and eating places were now designed to attract respectable couples; and shopping, once merely a chore best left to women, was increasingly seen as a leisure activity that both men and women could enjoy. These higher romantic expectations, and this greater

'WALLPAPER WOULD DISCOLOUR AND CURL'

NOT ALL overcrowded homes were unhappy ones. In his autobiography, *George*, the actor and playwright Emlyn Williams recalls the little house in Wales where he lived as a boy in the 1920s.

❝ Its great drawback, confirmed by the winter, was that it was below sea-level; certain days, through the grid under the tap, water would well remorselessly up and flood the yard. Wallpaper would discolour and curl dismally away from crumbling mortar, and three months after I had stored my *Companions* away in the parlour cupboard, I found them mouldily stuck together for ever...

But the kitchen was small and not hard to warm, and became the living-room for the five of us. It was dominated by a handsome oak dresser, the only Treuddyn heirloom...Under the little window which framed back yard and embankment, the hoary horsehair sofa; between sofa and fire – oven and grate immaculate with black-lead and gleaming irons – my father's chair, hard but with arms; behind him a fretwork rack...for his spills, and the cupboard for crockery and groceries. Under the stairs, which occupied a quarter of the room, the "spench", a dark place of crannies which would have been a huddle of muddle but for my mother's unconquerable sense of order. Besides a sack of potatoes, it stored – on a dozen nails and in rejected boxes on their sides, each in its appointed place – boots, shoe box complete with rags, brushes and polish, tools, Dad's shaving tackle, old newspapers to be sold to the chip shop at a penny a bundle, paraffin can, saucepan, frying pan, washbasin and an immense earthenware breadpan. On the high mantelpiece over the brass airing rail, the tea caddy faces, grimmer every year and by now bursting with laces and string. Hanging from the ceiling, the oil lamp.

Next to the spench, against the stairs, a small round table where Mam stood ministering at a chipped marble bread-slab, or washing up.... Behind the back door, on one nail, the coats of the whole family... ❞

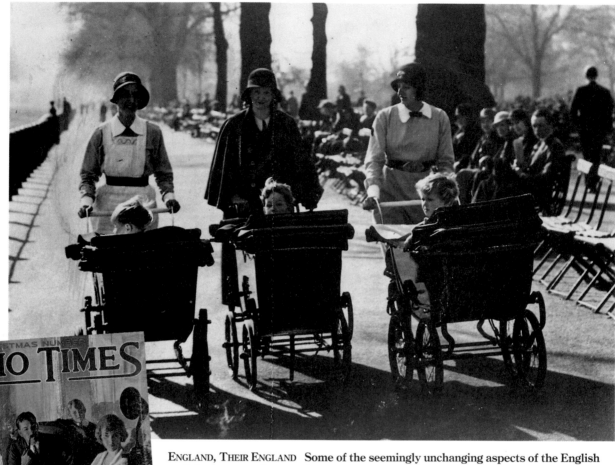

ENGLAND, THEIR ENGLAND Some of the seemingly unchanging aspects of the English social scene: nannies parade with their prams (above) and families gather around the fireside (left), listening to the early evening radio programmes.

intimacy, together with feeling isolation from the old communities, imposed strains on married life. The number of divorces increased greatly, and not just because they were easier to obtain. In Britain and the Protestant parts of Europe the divorce rate was three times its 1900 level. In the United States by the end of the 1920s one in every six marriages was terminated in the courts, and the complaints were not just for desertion, adultery and cruelty: women turned to the divorce courts because their husbands were inadequate providers of the good things of life; husbands because their wives, after marriage, had ceased to be 'fun' or because they were not prepared to settle down as mothers and homemakers. But for society as a whole the family,

consisting of a husband and wife with two or three children living rather closely together, had become the norm. This was the image advertisers used to promote products from boot polish to breakfast cereals.

HOUSING AND FAMILY LIFE

Family life was shaped to a great extent by the degree of wealth or the lack of it, and by the housing available. The very rich still lived on the grand scale familiar from the 19th century, moving between town

---

A MEASURE OF SUPPORT

In 1935 the American George Gallup conducted his first opinion poll for the advertising firm Young and Rubicam. Within a year Gallup polls were predicting results of elections and measuring public opinion on major issues, as they have done ever since.

HIGH SOCIETY The motor car gave freedom; society ladies picnic on Long Island, 1926.

and country houses according to the season and employing the traditional range of servants from butler, housekeeper and lady's maid, down through footmen and parlour maids to the scullery maid and the bootboy. In 1930 the father of the Woolworth heiress, Barbara Hutton, then 18, applied in her name for a private railway car. (It would cost upwards of $3 million in today's values):

'In addition to our apartments on Fifth Avenue, my father maintains a home in Palm Beach, a plantation and shooting preserve near Charleston, South Carolina, and we usually spend summers at Newport,

HUMBLE HOME A coal miner in the north of England at his evening meal. His hands are washed, but not his face.

Rhode Island, when not abroad. During the next few years I anticipate that my father will entertain me extensively at Palm Beach, New York, Charleston and Newport, and our family will make frequent trips between these places, and I expect to accompany them with guests of my own.'

Even the children of less fabulously wealthy families were brought up by nannies, nursery maids and governesses, and boys especially were sent away to school or educated by tutors. As a result, relations between parents and children could be quite remote and formal. Jessica Mitford, daughter of Lord Redesdale, though she and her sisters were taught at home by their mother, recalls: 'In my earliest memory of them Muv and Farve were actually as tall as the sky and as large as Marble Arch, and were somewhat more powerful than King and Parliament rolled into one.'

Some children saw their mothers only for an hour or two in the course of a day, their fathers even less, and were emotionally closer to favourite servants. Large houses offered separate bedrooms and dressing rooms for husband and wife and were frequently filled with guests, so that couples were not obliged to live more intimately than they wished.

Since the war, however, many of the formerly rich had been forced to scale down their households. Higher taxes, higher wages for servants – and the difficulty of obtaining good servants at all – made it troublesome to keep up large houses in both town and country. The face of London's best address, Mayfair, changed in the 1920s as many of the great town houses of the old aristocracy were torn down and replaced by hotels, offices and apartment buildings. A similar fate befell New York's famous avenues and the mansions of the 19th century's 'Robber barons', which had come to seem unfashionably ostentatious as well as expensive to maintain. Young upper-class couples shocked their parents by moving into apartments or quite modest houses with only one or two servants and generally living in a more middle-class fashion. At the same time, the suburban housing boom and better wages enabled large numbers of the less well-off to move up to a middle-class lifestyle, so that for the first time a large percentage of families were now living at broadly the same level.

One of the features that characterised middle-class family life was the fact that, though it was more intimate than the lives of the very rich or the old aristocracy, individual family members could enjoy a degree of privacy in their own rooms. On the other hand, at the lower end of the social scale it was impossible to be alone. Parents and children lived in close proximity, washing and dressing in the presence of others. In the homes of miners, for example, before pithead showers were introduced, the man of the house bathed in a tub in the family kitchen in water heated on the stove or the fire by his wife. In the countryside, in the homes of poor farmers or farmworkers, people bathed outside, or in the kitchen, on the rare occasions when they bathed at all, and never washed the whole body at one time. There was little

FEMINISTS The awareness and recognition of women's rights began to change traditional attitudes. Here, American feminists confer on an equal-rights campaign.

space for people's private possessions, few though these might be. Privacy between man and wife was almost impossible. Lovemaking took place within earshot of the children, although the French writer Leon Frapie records one couple, living together with their children in a one-room apartment, who sent the children to wait quietly on the stairway outside before engaging in lovemaking. His implication is that many couples did not trouble to be so discreet.

Many people in the interwar years lived in these cramped conditions, especially in countries such as France, Spain and Italy, which lagged behind in living standards and in improved public housing. It would be wrong to suppose that they led unhappy lives as a result – in the warmer parts of Europe and the United States they simply spent more of their time out of doors – but there was a great gulf between their lives and those of their newly prosperous working-class and middle-class contemporaries who could afford more spacious accommodation, in houses with separate bedrooms and kitchens and bathrooms with hot and cold running water.

The kitchen gave the woman of the house her own domain, separate from the other activities of the family, while her husband pursued his hobbies in the garden, the garage or the basement. The family still ate together around the table, and they spent their evening leisure time together in the living room, now carpeted and furnished with sofa and armchairs.

From the mid 1920s on, the favourite evening entertainment for millions of families was listening to the radio. The wireless set, still a large piece of equipment until portables appeared in the late 1930s, dominated the living room. It had become almost a member of the new, smaller family. It offered, for the first time, a medium for news and entertainment that whole families could share with each other, and with the whole nation. It was to cheer many lives in the hard Depression years. Americans from 1933 on could listen to President Roosevelt's 'fireside chats' and the Australian writer Patsy Adam-Smith, brought up in the bush in those years, recalls listening to the hugely popular family serial *Dad and Dave:*

'We loved *Dad and Dave*. After all, they were just gentle caricatures of us bushwhackers, or "bushies" as they say today. Our family had the only wireless in the area, and every weeknight people came from miles around by horse, bike, cart and beaten-up tin lizzies to

TWENTIES TYPISTS Schools of shorthand typing flourished in the interwar years, reflecting the seemingly endless demand for skilled women typists (above). Many women's magazines (right), however, still emphasised married bliss.

listen in with us. At 7 pm we'd hear the music start up – you didn't turn on until then in case the battery went flat: we were 20 miles from the nearest town where we could get it recharged. We'd crowd into the "front" room, up close to the big speaker, and through the static we'd hear the voices that made us laugh or cry or tremble. *Dad and Dave* did all those things to us. I'll always remember when Dad was about to lose Snake Gully, his farm, in a drought. He came in and said: "Well, Mum, it's come to this." I'll never forget Mum's reply: "Dad, we started from nothing and we'll start from nothing again." As all of us bush people crowded around, knowing what that meant, the tears poured down our faces.'

A WOMAN'S PLACE

The contribution that women had made to the war effort was now generally recognised. And it was this, rather than the activities of militant suffragettes, that led to their being granted the vote in the 1920s and to the improvement of their legal standing. Married women were now free to dispose of their own property and had rights similar to men's in divorce suits. Trade union pressure led to them losing the jobs that many had held in the war years, for example in transport, printing, munitions and engineering. But more women than ever now worked outside the home, especially in secretarial and clerical work, in the retail trade, in textiles and in the newer light industries.

Those who previously would have had no choice but to go into domestic service could – and did – opt for better paid work, with brighter company, fixed hours and less need to be so deferential to their employers. A shorthand typist or factory worker in Britain could earn £2 a week, her equivalent in the United States rather more, compared with the few shillings earned by maids in private houses. Women from prosperous middle-class families were now expected to find an occupation of some kind before marriage. Educated women found the professions open to them, and the numbers of women lawyers and doctors increased sharply. Women began, albeit in small numbers, to enter their countries' legislatures, and to become mayors and magistrates.

This experience undoubtedly gave women in general a greater self-confidence. 'They appear more alert, more critical of the conditions under which they work', the British magazine *New Statesman* noted. 'They have a keener appetite for experience and pleasure.' They were also far less burdened with childbearing – observers of the time noted how much *younger* working-class women in particular looked. But, society was still male-dominated. Women tended to find employment in the lesser-skilled jobs or in work specifically seen as feminine such as nursing, cleaning or dressmaking, in secretarial jobs or as waitresses or shop assistants. Where they did do the same work as men, they were almost invariably paid less, often only half as much. One result of this was that when employers laid off labour they tended to lay off the men first, as there was more of a saving to be had on wages. Although more women were now going to universities and entering the professions, they frequently found themselves socially excluded or discriminated against. The British novelist and social reformer Winifred Holtby, in her book *Women*, published in 1934, wrote:

'The young probationer, scuttling down the long corridors of the hospital; the aspirant to the hotel business counting linen in the basement storeroom; the junior reporter encountering upon the stone staircase of the great newspaper building the boss of the concern, and the factory hand watching the proprietor of the works drive off to a board meeting – these leaders, these field marshals whose baton she does not, she feels, carry in her knapsack, are not women.'

Despite the new opportunities opening up to them, most young women still looked forward to marriage as the fulfilment of life. Romantic novels and magazine stories still presented the wedding day as the end rather than the beginning of the story; women's magazines, which came into their own in the interwar years (the most successful British one, *Woman*, was selling three-quarters of a million copies by 1939), put far more emphasis on home and family than on work, careers or the possibilities of an independent life. After marriage, women came under pressure of a new kind, especially from advertisers: to maintain their youthful looks much longer than had been expected before. 'Keep young and beautiful, if you want to be loved', were the slightly bullying words of a popular song of the period. When the message was repeated to French women by the

WORK AND LEISURE Women making powder puffs, Long Island, about 1930 (above), and married women enjoying teatime out of doors (right), from an advertisement of the same period.

magazine *Marie Claire* soon after its launch in 1937, one middle-aged reader wrote to the editor to protest that it was asking too much of women: keeping one's looks had not been part of the marriage contract in earlier times. But the trend was not to be reversed, especially as the fashion for lighter clothing at that time emphasised the shape of the body more than in the past. Millions were spent on advertising, not only cosmetics and perfume, but also soaps, shampoos, deodorants, skin creams, toothpaste, diet aids and mineral waters. The cult of slimness and good looks was part of the new consumer society, but it did make women of the poorer classes more aware of the desirability of good diet, cleanliness, and healthy teeth and hair.

Though many women now worked outside the home it was only in Britain and the USA that they did so to any extent after marriage. Even in those countries relatively few did, and there was little likelihood of men sharing the 'women's work' of the home. In Germany, and in other countries too when the Depression struck, there was considerable hostility towards married women who worked – they were depriving men of all-too-scarce jobs. In Germany they were known as *Doppelverdiener*, those who brought home a second wage-packet, and in the German postal service the number of married women employed was actually reduced between 1922 and 1923 from 2718 to 21. The largest percentage of working women in Germany were still those helping in small family businesses. There was also a strong traditional view, shared by many women as well as men, that a married woman's duty, and greatest source of fulfilment, was to make a cosy home for her husband and raise his children.

This view was heavily emphasised by the Nazis. Their propaganda urged women to have large families to strengthen the Fatherland. Women with more than four children were awarded medals – bronze for a mother of four or five, silver for those with six or seven, gold for those with eight or more – and artists

MEDALS FOR MOTHERS During the Nazi period, mothers were awarded crosses of bronze, silver or gold (right), according to the number of children they bore. Crosses are awarded at a ceremony in Berlin (above).

were instructed not to depict German families with less than four children. An article in the newspaper *Volkischer Beobachter* in 1934 summarised the ideal: 'We must set this as an attainable goal: the mother should be able to dedicate herself entirely to her children, the wife to her husband; the unmarried girl should be trained only for those jobs that are compatible with her female character. Beyond this, employment should be left to the man.'

CHILDHOOD AND YOUTH

With more leisure time and fewer children, parents were able to bestow more care, affection and attention on those they had. As child labour became a thing of the past, as wages improved and as housing became

READY, STEADY, GO   A makeshift-scooter race in the USA. Children's toys were often simple and homemade.

less crowded, the notion of childhood as a time for play and education became a reality for many working-class families for the first time. Parent-child relations were less formal – except among that tiny minority who still employed nannies and governesses, and sent their children away to school at any early age. Discipline, though firmer than today, was less strict than in Victorian times. As well as carrying articles on fashion and cooking, women's magazines devoted space to child care, popularising new ideas about the social and emotional needs of children as distinct from their physical and spiritual welfare. But children were kept under the surveillance of parents or neighbours, and where families farmed, or ran businesses from home, they were expected to work. The French sociologist Yvonne Verdier recalled her childhood in the 1920s:

'When my grandmother saw us doing nothing, she would say: "Here girl, here's a piece to hem." . . . I milked the cows, fed the chickens and rabbits, and in the morning did a little housekeeping. We had a dozen cows, and mama and I had to take care of them. I could milk four an hour, mama maybe five. During the summer I always rose before dawn. From noon until two we hoed the beet and carrot patch. I was doing all this work by age 12.'

When she was 17, she recalled: 'I assure you, no boy could come near me. My father wouldn't let them. When I went dancing in 1925 he was always around, and when he called me, I had best not dawdle. If I was

dancing, I left the boy standing there and ran, because my father had already left.'

American parents might be more indulgent than Yvonne Verdier's, but, as the American magazine writer Dorothy Dix put it in the 1930s: 'Childhood is so short and the balance of life is so long. At best, a mother can satin-pad the world for her children for a few years. Then they are bound to face realities, and it is a bitter price they must pay for her folly in turning them into weaklings, instead of strong men and women.' And, as the American historian William Manchester recalled:

'One of the first lessons a child learned – because it would be a future asset when he applied for a job – was the importance of personal appearance. "Sit up *straight*!" he was told, and "Here's fifteen cents, go get a

BOY RACER   For sheer ingenuity, the average ten-year-old boy was hard to beat. This is an American 'land yacht' of the 1920s.

haircut." He might prefer a Flexible Flyer sled or a Simplex typewriter, but what he got first was an $8.95 blue serge suit comprising a coat, vest and knickers, and a pair of black $2.95 Gold Bond shoes. He wore them Sundays and on the first day of each semester, when every mother examined her son like a sergeant going over his men before a white-glove inspection.'

The streets of residential areas, especially in the suburbs where many people now lived, were safe for the children to play in, and municipal playgrounds were built in the poorer parts of towns, but children were expected to spend more leisure time with their parents than today – not only in the home but on visits to the cinema, weekend excursions and family holidays. At home children also had their own early evening radio programmes: *Tom Mix*, *The Lone Ranger* and *Little Orphan Annie* in the United States and in Britain the long-running favourites of BBC Children's Hour, such as *Toy-Town* and readings and dramatisations of much-loved books such as *The Jungle Books* or *The Wind in the Willows*. Or they played ping-pong, parlour games, card and board games or made jigsaw puzzles. During the Depression years in the United States, family recreation of this kind actually increased.

Among the huge growth of consumer goods now available were toys, games and books for children. There were now children's comics in the United States and Britain; cheaply printed on pulp paper, they had few equivalents elsewhere in Europe. The Americans had long had children's comic pages in their Sunday newspapers but the first American comic book, *Famous Funnies,* appeared in 1934. The British had *Chips* and *The Rainbow* and later the *Beano*, the *Dandy*, the *Wizard, Rover, Hotspur* and *Champion*, and comics about favourite characters from the world of radio and film comedy. The new comics frequently adopted a mildly rebellious tone that would have been unacceptable in earlier times.

Children's books were now much less moralistic than those of the Victorian era, as it was now assumed that children were naturally innocent rather than naturally sinful. However, boys' books in particular placed a heavy emphasis on heroism, bravery and other manly achievements.

LESSON In the 1930s nursery (above), a nanny helps a little girl to read her book. If she does well, she may be allowed to play, perhaps with a Mickey Mouse board game (right).

Many of the children's books of the period were of poor literary quality, but some enduring classics were produced. British children could enjoy A.A. Milne's *Winnie-the-Pooh* (1926), and the child-centred adventure novels of Arthur Ransome. Richmal Crompton's *Just William* books and Enid Blyton's *Noddy* stories were also extremely popular at the time and, almost starting a whole new genre, the children's career novel – Noel Streatfield's *Ballet Shoes*.

The hitherto almost unbroken line of books by middle-class authors based on middle-class life was broken by Eve Garnett's *The Family from One End Street,* about the lives of slum children. In Britain there was also a vogue for books about boarding schools, particularly among middle and working-class

HITLER'S CHILDREN: YOUTH IN THE THIRD REICH

ONE of the earliest acts of the Nazi party when they came to power in Germany in 1933 was to ban all youth organisations (except, for a while, Catholic ones) or to absorb them into the party's own youth movements. By the end of that year, 47 per cent of boys between the ages of 10 and 14 were in the *Deutsches Jungvolk* and 38 per cent of boys between 14 and 18 were in the Hitler Youth. A smaller amount of German girls were in the *Jungmädelbund* and the *Bund Deutscher Mädel*.

As long as membership was voluntary, the Hitler Youth offered a number of inducements: a wide range of sports and leisure activities and trips away from the restrictions of home. In addition, the uniform gave members opportunities, which some of them certainly enjoyed, for behaving arrogantly towards older people, such as parents and teachers. But the Nazi youth movements were devoted to indoctrination in the nationalist ideology and to the inculcation of military virtues. Paramount was loyalty to the Führer, and the young were encouraged to denounce anyone, parents included, heard expressing disloyal sentiments.

As pressure to join the Nazi youth movements increased during the 1930s, and discipline and surveillance became stricter, the enthusiasm of some of the young members began to wane. By the late 1930s, thousands of them were playing truant from the Hitler Youth and forming their own independent gangs with their own anti-Nazi, or non-Nazi, culture.

Some of these gangs belonged to larger groups known as 'The Edelweiss Pirates' and 'The Swing Youth'. The Edelweiss Pirate gangs, mainly boys aged between 14 and 18

WITH BANNERS HIGH! From early childhood, children were targeted by Nazi propaganda; this is from a Nazi nursery book.

with a few girls, wore distinctive clothing and badges, including the skull and crossbones. They relished beating up Hitler Youth patrols and 'Down with Hitler' and 'Eternal War on the Hitler Youth' were among the slogans they scrawled on the walls of German towns. They hitchhiked long distances, played guitars and sang protest songs.

Whereas the Edelweiss Pirates were mainly working class, the Swing Youth came from more privileged backgrounds. They rejected Nazi-approved music and devoted themselves to American jazz, swing and the jitterbug, along with collar-length hair, slovenly dress and free-wheeling sexual behaviour.

In 1939 membership of the Nazi Youth became compulsory. When war came, thousands of the non-Hitler youth group members were

sent to concentration camps and some of their leaders were hanged. Others worked in anti-Nazi resistance groups.

The National Socialists destroyed traditional working-class and middle-class culture among Germany's youth. But ironically, because what they offered as an alternative was so repressive and stifling they encouraged the growth of something very like today's youth culture.

TOMORROW'S SOLDIERS
Two *Jungvolk* in Hitler Youth uniform.

PLAYTIME Boys and girls come out to play in a Denver school playground. American schools were well-equipped.

boys who did not have to endure them, and who liked to dream about baiting the masters or toasting sausages before the study fire.

American children could enjoy the *Little House* novels of Laura Ingalls Wilder about pioneer life, and Will James's magical story about the horse *Smoky* (1926). Germany introduced the boy detective with Erich Kastner's *Emil and the Detectives* (1929). The French, though they had always lagged behind Germany and the Anglo-Saxon world in children's literature, gave the world Jean de Brunhoff's engaging Babar the Elephant stories and, from Belgium, from the 1930s on, came the incomparable strip-cartoon adventures of Tintin.

BOYS AND GIRLS

Girls were dressed in distinctly feminine styles, usually in floral-print frocks and with their hair in ringlets, and they were expected to stay clean. Only the upper classes, or those too poor to have much choice, permitted girls to wear 'tomboyish' clothes. Until the age of 14 or 15, when boys made the 'right-of-passage' transition to long trousers, they invariably wore shorts in Britain, and shorts or knickerbockers in the United States and Europe. They were urged at least to try to maintain a respectable appearance, especially on Sundays, when best clothes were worn and boisterous behaviour out-of-doors was forbidden.

Pocket money, though given sparingly, went a long way. A penny or two would buy an ice cream, sweets or a chocolate bar or, for American children, a Horton's Dixie Cup or a Coke at the corner drugstore. It was the ambition of every boy to own a bicycle and most, eventually, did. Cheap clockwork toys were now being mass-produced and the better-off might be given train sets or construction sets as birthday or Christmas presents. But elaborate and expensive possessions were rare, and most boys still improvised their outdoor amusements with marbles and bat and ball, or homemade buggies and sledges. Children everywhere still chalked

CARS FOR BOYS Model cars were raced and collected by boys of all ages. These are American, from the late 1920s.

PLAYTIME Role-playing children of the 1930s. Parents of the time put great emphasis on good behaviour and encouraged neatness and tidiness.

hopscotch patterns on the pavement and acted out ritual playground games. In Britain they played 'conkers' or swapped the cards that came with cigarette packets; in the United States they collected the portraits of sporting heroes, such as Babe Ruth, on bubble-gum wrappers. Girls sang to routines with skipping ropes and played with their dolls, which had increasingly lifelike faces, hair and clothes.

The upbringing of children still emphasised unquestioningly the stereotypical gender roles of male and female. Girls were taught to sew and knit, and learned to cook by watching their mothers in the kitchen; boys helped their fathers chop wood or dig the garden or tinker with the family car. A survey conducted in the United States in 1931 found that most boys of eight years old wanted to be cowboys, aviators or army officers when they grew up; and girls wanted to be movie stars. By the age of 18, preferences had changed. Boys now wanted to be lawyers, electrical engineers or architects; while girls were training to be secretaries.

As the world moved into the Depression, hard times were reflected in children's lives. The Australian writer Patsy Adam-Smith remembers the thriftiness necessary in the late 1920s: 'The Christmas gift to buy for Dad was tailor-made cigarettes – a change from roll-your-own. Mum once went so far as to buy herself an overcoat from an advertisement at 2s 6d a week. We told her she looked "real flash". And she'd earned it. Most nights she would work for hours unpicking old clothes and remaking them for my sister Mick and me. We thought they looked as good as new.

We never envied the rich, their clothes and their cars. We didn't have much money, but in our way we were having a lot of fun . . . '

Helen Forrester, who spent her childhood in a Liverpool slum after her father had fallen on hard times, remembers how he learned how to make do:

'There were agencies in the town, he was told, which would provide the odd pair of shoes or an old blanket for a child. There were regimental funds willing to provide a little help to old soldiers. He gathered other scraps of information, which were revelations to a man who had never had to think twice about the basic necessities of life. An open fire, he was assured, could be kept going almost all day from the refuse of the streets, old shoes, scraps of paper, twigs, wooden boxes, potato peelings; if one was very ill or had a broken bone, the outpatients department of most of the local hospitals would give some medical care. Pawnbrokers would take almost anything saleable, and one could buy secondhand from them. Junk yards would sometimes yield a much needed pram wheel or a piece for an old bike.'

YOUTH AND YOUTH MOVEMENTS

Vast numbers of young people joined organised youth movements in the 1920s and 30s. In Britain and the United States membership of the Boy Scouts and the Cubs almost trebled between the wars, and the Girl Guides (or Girl Scouts) and Brownies, founded in 1910, had become the most popular organisation for girls by 1939. The Boy Scouts were successful even in Catholic France and in pre-Hitler Germany, where there was a cult of youth, around one in two boys and girls belonged to a youth organisation, such as sports clubs, church youth groups, the workers' youth movement, or the *Wandervogel* hiking clubs. The last of these were to become increasingly nationalistic in the 1920s, and all of them were either abolished after the Nazis came to power or subsumed into the Hitler Youth and its sister movement. In contrast, the beginnings of a teenage lifestyle were emerging in the United States, where children were given much more freedom and spending power.

HOME LIFE BETWEEN THE WARS

As the homes of the rich became smaller, those of the poor

were becoming more spacious and comfortable.

New workers' flats were changing the shape of family life.

For the middle classes, the home was increasingly a place in which to

display consumer goods and enjoy leisure activities,

especially listening to the wireless.

TOWNS AND HOUSES

Some critics sneered at the new suburban houses, but they offered a way of life that

ordinary people relished. The old Victorian slums were being cleared, and millions

were beginning to enjoy electricity and running water in their homes for the first time.

WHEREAS town centres had spread hugely in the previous hundred years, by the 1920s and 30s they were growing dramatically upwards instead. In the United States skyscrapers shot up in every major American city, and in New York's Grand Central district alone, the amount of office space multiplied by a factor of ten between 1918 and 1930. The centres of many European cities also changed, as 18th and 19th-century terraced houses and the mansions of the rich were torn down to make way for new office and apartment buildings. But what was new in this period was the enormous growth of public and subsidised private housing, especially in Britain and Germany. This had been prompted by a severe housing shortage after the war, and by a strong determination to clear or improve the worst of the Victorian slums.

In Germany an average of 200 000 dwellings were either built or renovated every year between 1920 and 1933. (In the prewar years the Nazis actually managed 300 000 per year, though they failed to keep up with a rising population and with heavy migration from the country to the towns.) In Britain 4 million flats and houses were built between 1918 and 1939 – about half of them for sale, and most of the rest rented from local authorities. Estates of workers' housing were constructed on a large scale, and improved public transport allowed people to live farther from their

SUPER **1933** HOMES

THE GROWING SUBURBS Suburban housing estates, like the one above in Sussex, proliferated. In Britain, the semi-detached house in mock-Tudor style (top left) was popular, although architectural critics often sneered at it.

SUNDAY IN THE SUBURBS **An English couple prepare for an outing. The house cost about £900, the car about £130.**

work, encouraging the growth of suburbs. Many areas around big cities, where in 1914 sheep had grazed or forests had grown, were now filled with housing developments. The growth of motor transport also led to strip development, especially along the new bypass roads, which the authorities tried to contain, for example by establishing statutory green belts in which building development was carefully controlled. The authorities also resumed the practice begun before the war of creating garden suburbs and new towns, such as Welwyn Garden City, founded in 1920, which aimed to offer a combination of modern housing and the benefits of clean air, recreation space and easy access to the countryside.

The downside to all this was that whereas Victorian housing developments had offered a mixture of housing for people on different income levels, these new developments tended to be zoned, actually reinforcing class differences. In Britain workers' flats were called tenements and named 'So-and-So's Buildings' after famous social reformers or figures in the Labour movement, while the apartment buildings that the well-to-do were moving into, as a consequence of higher taxes, increased labour costs and the subsequent need to close down their town houses, were given aristocratic, stately home-type names such as 'Albemarle House' or 'Clarendon Court'.

A MACHINE FOR LIVING IN **The ultramodern style never really caught on for domestic architecture.**

Meanwhile, middle-class people and the better-off workers were moving out into the new suburbs to enjoy the benefits of space and fresh air, so that increasingly only the poor or the rich lived in the centres of towns. Zoning into industrial, commercial and residential areas also had the effect of destroying many of the old neighbourhoods, with their familiar mixture of housing, shops and bars or cafés. Whether in council estates or suburban houses, people sometimes found themselves missing the sort of informal neighbourly contacts that the older urban housing had offered.

The workers' flats built in Weimar Germany and in Socialist Vienna were often well-designed, combining the new functionalist architectural ideas with healthy living conditions – and frequently offering communal services such as public laundries, restaurants, nursery schools and even tennis courts and swimming pools. But many found their austere lines, their departure from the human scale and their uniformity somewhat soulless. The National Socialists, in their public housing projections, favoured houses rather than flats, because these were thought to be more traditional and Germanic, and to symbolise the family rooted in the soil of the Fatherland. The flats they actually built were on average larger than the Weimar ones, reflecting their emphasis on large families, with rents beyond the means of the poorer classes. Workers' tenements in Britain tended to have a barrack-like dreariness – 'they look like pickle factories, but quite good pickle factories,' wrote Osbert Lancaster – though they were usually built well away from major traffic routes and had inner courtyards where children could play safely.

NEW HOUSING AND OLD

Those who could afford them preferred the detached or semidetached houses built in huge numbers from the mid 1920s onwards, sometimes with government subsidies. In 1925 a three-bedroomed house with its own garden in the London area could be bought for

WASHING DAY Clothes lines strung across the street were a common feature of poorer housing districts everywhere. This is Ambridge, near Pittsburgh, in the 1930s. Here, as elsewhere, the street was a focus for social life.

WALTER GROPIUS AND THE BAUHAUS

Germany was a world leader in the development of the austere, functional architectural style, known as International Modernism, that began to emerge in the early 1900s. One of the principal exponents of that style was the architect Walter Gropius (1883-1969); his first building, a factory, dates from 1911 to 1914, but already has the totally undecorated, geometrical appearance that did not become widespread in architecture until the 1950s.

One of the first acts of the new Weimar government in 1919 was the opening of the Bauhaus ('House of building') school of art and design. Gropius was its first director and the architect of the new buildings at Dessau that it moved into in 1926. It was based on the radically new principle that art and craftsmanship should be combined to produce the best possible design for industrial production in the machine age.

Subjects taught at the Bauhaus included carpentry, metalwork, pottery, weaving, graphics, typography, from 1927, architecture; instruction in each of these was given by two teachers, one an artist, the other a craftsman, and the teachers

included, apart from Gropius himself, some of the greatest artists and designers of the day: Paul Klee, Wassily Kandinsky, Lyonel Feininger, Laszlo Moholy-Nagy and Marcel Breuer. One of Gropius's finest achievements at this time was his contribution to an experimental estate at the Weissenhof near Stuttgart in 1927, but the influence of the Bauhaus on design and architecture generally was immense and worldwide.

The modernism of the Bauhaus was not popular in conservative and nationalist circles – one critic called it 'an enemy fortress in the midst of the Fatherland' – and it was closed down by the Nazis in 1933, when another influential modernist architect, Mies van der Rohe, was director. Gropius himself resigned as director in 1928 and in 1934 went to England, where he worked with the

BAUHAUS Walter Gropius, and a trend-setting metal and glass tablelamp from 1925.

British architect Maxwell Fry. One of their major collaborations was Village College at Impington in Cambridgeshire. In 1938 he went to the United States as professor of architecture at Harvard. Working with Marcel Breuer he designed the Harvard University Graduate Center, the University of Baghdad and the United States Embassy in Athens.

Gropius died in 1969.

**A NEW ARCHITECTURE
A 1920s Bauhaus-style housing estate near Stuttgart, designed by Mies van der Rohe and others.**

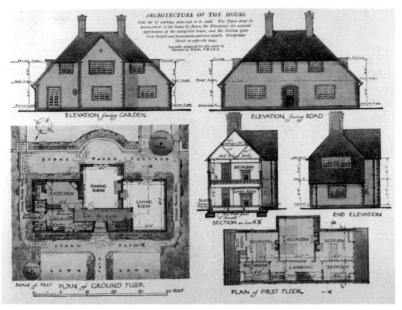

ARCHITECTURE OF THE HOUSE

ELEVATION *facing* GARDEN

ELEVATION *facing* ROAD

END ELEVATION

SECTION *on line* KB

PLAN *of* GROUND FLOOR

PLAN *of* FIRST FLOOR

DESIRABLE RESIDENCE The development of suburbs in Britain allowed those who could afford it the chance to choose a house to suit their needs.

£920, and elsewhere they were considerably cheaper, costing approximately twice the annual salary of a professional man. During the 1920s the London Underground advertised a new suburban development:

'Stake your claim at Edgware. Omar Khayyam's recipe for turning the wilderness into a paradise hardly fits an English climate, but provision has been made at Edgware of an alternative recipe which at least will convert pleasant, undulating fields into happy homes. The loaf of bread, the jug of wine and the book of verse may be got there cheaply and easily, and . . . a shelter which comprises all the latest labour-saving and sanitary conveniences.'

In the United States there was also a boom in suburban building development, partly fuelled by a sharp drop in the value of agricultural land and by the drift of former country dwellers to the cities. On the outskirts of the great cities such as New York, Chicago, Los Angeles and Detroit huge tracts of land were subdivided into housing plots. Some of the housing built on those plots was in the

AN ENGLISHMAN'S CASTLE

THE WRITER AND CARTOONIST Osbert Lancaster in his *Pillar to Post, the Pocket Lamp of Architecture*, published in 1938, describes the style of English suburban house he called 'By-Pass Variegated'.

❛ As one passes by, one can amuse one's self by classifying the various contributions which past styles have made to this infernal amalgam; here are some quaint gables culled from Art Nouveau surmounting a façade that is plainly Modernistic in inspiration; there the twisted beams and leaded panes of

Stockbroker's Tudor are happily contrasted with bright green tiles of obviously Pseudish origin; next door some terracotta plaques, Pont Street Dutch in character, enliven a white wood Wimbledon Transitional porch, making it a splendid foil to a red-brick garage that is vaguely Romanesque in feeling...

Notice the skill

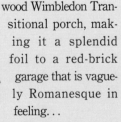

STYLISH TALENT Osbert Lancaster, the wit, writer, raconteur and artist.

with which the houses are disposed, that insures that the largest possible area of countryside is ruined with the minimum of expense; see how carefully each householder is provided with a clear view into the most private offices of his next-door neighbour and with what studied disregard of the sun's aspect the principal rooms are planned.

It is sad to reflect that so much ingenuity should have been wasted on streets and estates which will inevitably become the slums of the future. That is, if a fearful and more sudden fate does not obliterate them prematurely; an eventuality that does much to reconcile one to the prospect of aerial bombardment. ❜

CITY BLUES Fifth Avenue in 1926. Then, as today, crowds flocked to large cities for work or excitement.

form of 'garage dwellings' – temporary one-room shacks – but elsewhere, attractive suburbs were growing. Their promoters used flowery language to advertise their delights. 'To live at American Venice', wrote the promoters of a development on Long Island, 'is to quaff the very Wine of Life . . . A turquoise lagoon under an aquamarine sky! Beautiful Italian gardens! . . . And, ever present, the waters of the Great South Bay lapping lazily all day upon a beach as white and fine as the soul of a little child.' Like so many things, the boom collapsed in 1929, but the suburban expansion of the 1920s had awakened a desire to live in conditions of space and freedom, with easy access to city centres – an ambition still widespread among people in the industrialised world.

What these new flats and houses had in common was electricity, hot and cold running water and separate kitchens or kitchenettes, bathrooms and lavatories.

Conservative newspapers joked

SUBURBAN BLISS Many people aspired to live in tranquil suburbs.

about the new bathrooms for the working classes, suggesting that they would keep coal or rabbits in them, but they were one of the factors that led to a marked improvement in the general health of the population. In the older houses, in rural areas, and in countries such as France, where the housing revolution did not take place until after the Second World War, many people rarely washed more than their hands and faces. The new bathrooms had mirrors, previously a rarity, and hot and cold running water, which encouraged people to make use of these facilities much more often than they had previously.

The modern kitchen was a great boon to young women moving out of cramped accommodation in the older tenements, though it demanded a change in living habits for many people used to the old style of combined kitchen-and-living room in which family life had mostly been spent. That the new flats also had

47

RURAL PEACE While towns were being transformed, the country remained largely unchanged. This is rural Dorset.

separate bedrooms was in itself a considerable advance, for many former slum-dwellers were used to living in one or two rooms, with two or more children to a bed.

Although much of it was being refurbished, most people still lived in the older housing stock. For many it meant back-to-back houses, as in the North of England, or tenement flats with outside lavatories, often shared with others, cold water only, or no piped water at all. In Liverpool in 1932, a hundred families were still living in cellars. In Birmingham alone there were still 40 000 back-to-backs. In Manchester the housing pioneer Sir Ernest Simon described one slum dwelling he had seen:

'The general appearance and condition of this house inside are very miserable. It is a dark house and the plaster on the passage walls, in particular, was in a bad condition. There is no sink or tap in the house; they are in the small yard, consequently in frosty weather the family is without water. In this house live a man and wife, and seven children, ranging from 15 to 1, and a large, if varying, number of rats.'

Housing like this could still be found in cities throughout Europe and America. A survey in Nazi Germany in 1937 showed that of 2000 working-class homes 96 per cent had no bathrooms, 22 per cent had no direct access to a water supply and 14 per cent had no electricity. This was also true in rural areas, even in America, where by 1939 only 10 per cent of farmhouses had electricity, 90 per cent had no baths or showers and 75 per cent had no indoor plumbing. By 1939 over two-thirds of all British households had electric light (but probably fewer elsewhere in Europe). The remainder still relied on gas or paraffin lamps. Overcrowding was still a problem. Although conditions

A PUBLIC DANGER
A French magazine of the 1920s asks: 'Isn't it time to replace these breeding-grounds of tuberculosis with healthy homes?'

ART DECO AND MODERNISM These styles caught the imagination and were used extensively in Europe and America, especially for public buildings. The Vaudeville Brasserie, Paris (above), is still in use, as is the De La Warr Pavilion at Bexhill-on-Sea on Britain's south coast.

were steadily improving, in 1931 in England and Wales 35 per cent of the population still lived more than two to a room, and the situation was similar in most of the towns of Europe.

Architects like Le Corbusier in France, Frank Lloyd Wright in America and Walter Gropius, creator of the Bauhaus, in Germany, were now creating the 'modernist' style in architecture, but few of their designs had actually got beyond the drawing board. Only a handful of private houses, some apartment buildings and some public buildings such as London's

newer underground stations represented the international modernist style in its purest form.

Modern steel-frame building methods and materials, such as concrete, steel and glass, were being used increasingly, and the Art Deco style was appearing in some new commercial buildings, such as department stores. Cinema builders favoured the 'modernistic' style, influenced by science fiction and designed, especially when combined with neon lighting, to be dramatic rather than purely functional; they also used 'Egyptian' or even 'Babylonian' motifs. The modernist idea of designing according to function, with minimal decoration, was also influencing some new office and apartment buildings, especially on the continent. But older styles, the neoclassical and even the Gothic, were still strongly favoured. Builders who were now offering new houses for sale tended to give people what they wanted: and what most people

AT HOME IN THE 1930S Many homes had wirelesses and gramophones, but the piano was still a common feature.

wanted was not the geometric lines of modernist architecture but a reminder of older fashions. In the suburbs of the United States they wanted something that hinted at a Colonial farmhouse (with attached garage) or a Spanish hacienda; in Canada and Australia something of the England, Ireland or Scotland that their ancestors had come from; and in Germany some memory of an ancestral home in the forest or the mountains. Architects might talk of houses as 'machines for living in', but people wanted homes that reflected their dreams.

The English suburban house, much mocked by the aesthetes and the critics of the time, might have steel-framed windows, but it also had pebbledashed walls, 'Tudor' timber-

CLEAN SWEEP A German housewife tries out her new vacuum cleaner, still a novelty in the 1930s.

work, decorative porches and sunrise patterns in mass-produced stained glass let into the front door, and just enough individuality to justify giving it a name of its own such as 'Dunroamin' or 'The Elms' or 'Mon Repos'. With its large garden, offering space for greenhouses, garden sheds and garages, the suburban house offered much that people desired and, despite the critics, has withstood the test of time.

INSIDE THE HOUSE

A new house built in the 1920s or 30s and lived in, say, by a school teacher or a small shopkeeper would have looked from the outside much as it does today; it might even have had a car parked outside it, particularly in America. (In Germany by 1932 there were eight private cars for every 1000 people; in Britain about 35; and in America there were 183.) Although house ownership was increasingly common, especially in Britain, most homes were rented. Inside, today's visitor would be struck more by what was not there than by what was. There were no electric blankets, automatic dish-

'No Trouble at All'
Electric appliances (left) began to invade the kitchen in the 1920s. Heatproof glassware (above) also made its appearance.

washers, clothes driers, vinyl floors, hi-fi sets (gramophones were hand-wound), home freezers, tape recorders, electric hair driers, air-conditioning units or, except in a tiny handful of homes by the late 1930s, television sets. The kitchen would have had a gas cooker, by the late 1930s possibly an electric one, but, except in the United States, probably not a refrigerator and almost certainly not a washing machine. Even in the United States, the refrigerator was still for many people an 'ice box', filled with ice supplied by the iceman, who was notified how many pounds were needed by a card placed in the kitchen window. Electric toasters and vacuum cleaners were a luxury for all but a few in the 1920s, and still not common by 1939.

Only a minority of households had telephones: in 1932 there were 52 for every 1000 people in Germany, 165 for every 1000 American households; Herbert Hoover, Roosevelt's predecessor, was the first American president to have one on his desk. In Britain the familiar red public telephone kiosk, designed by Sir Giles Gilbert Scott, was introduced in 1935.

Housework between the wars was still done by hand. Carpets, for most people, still had to be taken outside and beaten with specially designed wickerwork beaters. The laundry was still done in a tub with a washboard, wrung in a mangle and hung out to dry, generally on a Monday. (The poor went to public washhouses, which were popular meeting places for women otherwise tied to the home.) Most people did the ironing using a simple iron that had been heated on the stove or fire. But, even for those who could afford labour-saving devices, women's work was no easier, since conforming to new standards of hygiene and interior decoration actually took more time rather than less.

New houses had electric fires in the bedrooms, but houses were still mainly heated by stoves or open coal fires or, in the United States, by basement furnaces, which had to be lit first thing in the morning and regularly stoked. Coal was delivered and emptied into bunkers; American homes used 400 million tons of it every winter. Older tenement houses in Britain still had cast-iron stoves with ovens on each side of the fire and hot plates on top, which had to be kept bright with blacking. Domestic central heating in the modern sense was virtually unknown.

FURNISHING THE HOME

Fashions in furniture had changed radically. The Exhibition of Decorative Arts in Paris in 1925, which launched the Art Deco style, had an enormous international influence. The well-to-do, especially the younger well-to-do, swept out the over-decorated clutter regarded as desirable by their grandparents, and went almost to the opposite extreme. Furniture had clean,

THE WONDERFUL FUTURE

Predictions about the future in the 1920s and 30s were

sometimes accurate, sometimes hilariously wrong.

WORLD'S FAIR Spectators on a circular walkway marvel at 'Democracity', a miniature three-dimensional landscape, at the 1939 World Fair.

IN 1939 thousands of Americans and visitors from overseas, including King George VI of Great Britain, flocked to New York for the World's Fair of that year.

Its theme was 'Building The World of Tomorrow', and it was seen as the culmination, on the eve of world war, of two decades of speculation about the sort of future that the rapid developments made in science and technology might soon bring. The fair offered a wide range of attractions, including a robot called Elektro that could smoke and recite the Lord's Prayer in 300 languages. However, the most successful exhibit was General Motors' Futurama, created by the stage designer Norman Bel Geddes. 28 000 customers per day sat down in armchairs on a moving conveyor to look down on a vast scale model of what the America of the 1960s would look like. It would be a world carefully zoned into residential, commercial and industrial areas, its cities linked by seven-lane super highways. There would be office and apartment buildings 1500 ft (457 m) high, but many Americans would live in pleasant villages where they would work in the one-product factories, powered by atomic energy or liquid air, and grow their own food. Each village would have its own airport. Houses would be light and disposable. Work would be so mechanised that people would be able to devote most of their increased spare time to leisure and education. Cars would cost $200 and have air-conditioning.

Ever since the end of the 19th century people had become aware that science

WONDER STORIES 1930s science-fiction magazines offered imaginative visions of the future.

and technology were changing the shape of everyday life, and would do so even more dramatically in the future. The idea of constant change, and speculation about a greatly altered future, were features that made the 20th century different from earlier ages accustomed only to permanence or to slow and gradual development. Advertisements of the 1930s were full of references to 'the car of the future' or 'the home of the future'.

The new popular habit of thinking about the future coincided with the availability of cheap printing and gave rise, especially in America, to illustrated hobby magazines which devoted much of their space to the subject. Most of the projections were optimistic, especially in the gloomy 1930s, when there was a kind of 'nostalgia for the future'. They saw science and technology as a means of freeing men and women from the tyranny of labour, curing disease, and solving the problems that had created the miseries of the Depression. However, some of them were doom-laden, foreseeing a future in which machinery would enslave and dehumanise human beings. A superb example of the pessimistic

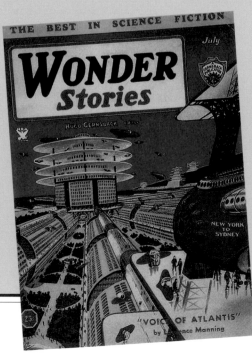

THE BEST IN SCIENCE FICTION

July

WONDER Stories

HUGO GERNSBACK Editor

NEW YORK TO SYDNEY

"VOICE OF ATLANTIS" by Laurence Manning

THINGS TO COME Visions of cities of the future were inspired by American skyscrapers, as in Fritz Lang's film *Metropolis* (above), sometimes in the shape of electrical components, as in this science-fiction illustration (right).

view was Fritz Lang's classic German film of 1926, *Metropolis* – inspired by seeing the skyscrapers of Manhattan – in which men and women laboured in a subterranean world under the gleaming towers of a magical city of the future.

A leading figure among the speculators about future technology was Hugo Gernsback, sometimes called the 'father of science fiction', who published a series of hobby magazines including *Science and Technology*. In 1926 Gernsback launched the first science-fiction magazine, *Amazing Stories*, which was to spawn many imitators in the 1930s. Its August 1928 issue saw the first appearance of Buck Rogers, who was to rocket to stardom in comic-strip form and then on radio, and to compete with Flash Gordon as the most popular science-fiction hero of the 1930s. During the 1930s a wide range of magazines, notably *Modern Mechanix*, devoted their covers to spectacular paintings of cities and machines of the future with accompanying articles inside. In 1932 *Popular Mechanics* carried an article written by Winston Churchill, MP, entitled *'Fifty Years Hence'*, in which the future British prime minister predicted that 'startling developments lie already just beyond our fingertips in the breeding of human beings and the shaping of human nature . . . the production of such beings may well be possible within fifty years . . . they will not be made, but grown under glass.'

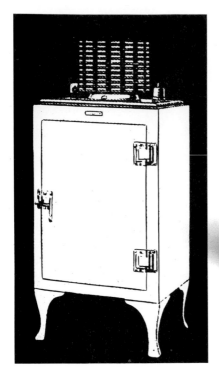

MACHINES AT HOME A 1938 TV (above). The picture was viewed through a mirror set in the raised lid. A 1931 refrigerator (left), with freezer unit on top.

simple lines. It was made of natural light-coloured woods or painted in fashionable pastel shades or in black, grey or white. Rooms were kept sparsely furnished, their walls distempered in monochrome. (Wallpaper had been unobtainable in the war years because of paper rationing and was out of fashion in the 1920s.) Fabrics had simple geometric or wild primitive patterns, influenced by 'jazz' motifs, Byzantine art or the richly coloured pagan designs of Diaghilev's Russian Ballet.

'Ornaments' of any kind were despised. Good taste dictated that any objets d'art or pictures should be carefully chosen and positioned – to be 'amusing' if possible. The fashion-conscious employed the help of the interior designer – a new profession – to combine antiques or primitive art with tubular steel and glass furniture. Many of the rich had converted their town houses into flats or had moved into new apartments: the 'Bright

GERMAN TELEPHONE In 1932 there were 52 telephones for every 1000 people in Germany. In the USA it was considerably more.

Young Things' restyled the living rooms of these flats, clearing the floors and installing cocktail bars, as if for an endless party.

But only a minority could afford to follow fashions in the furnishing of their homes. Most people still had the furniture they had bought or inherited in the 1900s or earlier, and many of the homes of older or poorer people still had a late 19th-century look. Ordinary people who could afford to buy new furniture favoured, as with their houses, a style that harked back to earlier times, and this was what the mass-producers of furniture on the whole provided. 'Jacobethan' and Regency styles were popular in England in the 1920s and 30s, and mahogany veneers were preferred to natural wood finishes. Though younger people were losing the Victorian impulse to cover every surface with tasselled velvet, embroidery or crocheted linen, or with vases, aspidistras and gewgaws of every kind, most homes of the 1920s and 30s still had comfortable clutter. Wallpaper came back into fashion in the mid 1930s, and there was even something of a Victorian revival.

Many attempts were made, especially at the Bauhaus in Germany, to combine the best in modern design with the mass-production process in furniture, ceramics and furnishing textiles, but at the popular level of factory production there was also a marked decline in the quality of design and manufacture: a tendency to cheap flashiness, which contrasted poorly with the best examples of traditional furniture and household crockery.

Changing tastes and the increasing availability of cheap mass-produced furniture *had* changed the look of most interiors by the mid 1930s. The main bedroom of any middle-class or prosperous working-class home would now have a glass-topped dressing table with a mirror, probably matching the wardrobe. The family sitting room would have an electric light-shade attached to the ceiling, carpeted floors, simple curtains rather than the elaborate drapes of the Victorian era, and 'occasional tables' for lamps and coffee trays. In Britain there would be a faceted mirror above the mahogany

FASHIONABLE INTERIOR Those who could afford it often employed an interior designer. This is the 1930s dining room of Robert Mallet-Stephens' home in France. He was a distinguished interior designer of that time.

FADS AND CRAZES BETWEEN THE WARS

THE 1920s was a great period for fads and crazes. One of the earliest was the pogo stick, a pole with a spring at the bottom end and a cross bar for the feet, designed to allow the user to move quite rapidly along in a series of jumps. A pogo-stick championship organised by the *Daily News* was won by a boy who managed 1600 jumps in 15 minutes and covered 600 yards (549 m) in 8 minutes.

Then there was the craze, which started in the English-speaking clubs of Shanghai and spread from there to the United States, for the Chinese game of mah-jong.

In 1922 there was a craze for a little gambling toy known as 'Put and Take'. This was a six-sided spinning top generally made of brass, each side engraved with instructions to 'Put one' or 'Take two' or 'Take all'. Players put money into a pool, spun the top and then followed the instructions on the side of the top that fell uppermost. For a few months

FLAT RACE In the 1920s, according to the caption, racing on wooden horses was 'A new feature in the Mayfair homes of society beauties'.

people were playing the game everywhere; then the craze died as suddenly as it had begun.

At about the same time there was a widespread fad in both Europe and the United States for the self-healing technique devised by a Frenchman named Emile Coué. It required the daily recitation of the words: 'Every day, and in every way I am getting better and better.'

The crossword puzzle craze originated in the United States in 1924 and most newspapers began to carry a daily crossword.

There were probably fewer fads and crazes in the more serious days of the 1930s, but there was one for the Yo-yo, thought to have originated in South America, where a wooden wheel which, with a skilful flick of the wrist, could be made to run up and down the string rolled round it.

GAMESMEN One of the crazes of the interwar years involved throwing and catching a ping-pong ball with a motor-car horn.

PLAYTIME A group of Washington ladies at mah-jong in 1923.

CHEER UP Mickey Mouse brightens a child's bedroom (left), but there is no sign of him in the château bedroom (above) of the Baroness de Rothschild.

mantel of the tiled fireplace. Prominent in the room would be a wireless set in a Bakelite plastic or 'modernistic' wooden case. Most of all, the room would have a 'three-piece suite' of comfortably upholstered sofa or couch and matching armchairs – something unknown to the Victorians, and still at this time virtually unknown in rural Italy or France, where families still spent their indoor lives around the table. This last item, the upholstered armchair, became an unconscious symbol of the middle-class home comforts that most people were now enjoying, as can be seen from many of the advertisements of the period.

BESTSELLING BOARD GAME

The board game Monopoly was invented by unemployed engineer Charles Darrow during the American Depression. Darrow offered to sell the game to leading games manufacturers Parker Brothers, who initially rejected it. In 1935 he privately made 5000 sets, which were so successful that Parker Brothers reversed their decision.

Parker Brothers launched the game nationally for the 1935 Christmas season – and by January 1936 it had swept the United States; not long afterwards it had swept the world. Since its launch it has sold over 80 million sets, and the annual issue of Monopoly money exceeds the annual dollar output of the United States Treasury.

For substantial purchases – and especially for buying cars, furnishing their homes and buying domestic appliances – people had come to depend on hire-purchase schemes, which financed the great increase in consumer spending and helped to create a consumer society. In the United States, by the second half of the 1920s, 15 per cent of all retail sales were on an instalment basis.

THE PLEASURE OF SHOPPING

For the first time, shopping trips to the city centre for clothing and household goods became a major activity for large numbers of people, aided by public transport systems. Buses carried advertisements for consumer goods and railway companies advertised special shopping excursion fares. A day's shopping in town, followed by tea and a visit to the cinema, could now almost be described as a leisure activity, at least for middle-class women.

In the cities, the department stores had been established since the late 19th century, but their style of presentation was rather different from today's. In the smarter ones a shopwalker in a morning coat greeted customers at the main door and directed them to the department they required, where a floorwalker would summon an assistant to serve them. Most goods were not displayed on open shelves for customers to examine for themselves, but had to be asked for and brought out from cabinets or storerooms by assistants. Chairs were placed along the

CITY SHOPPING Big stores advertised extensively; this is one of many posters for the French *Au Bon Marché* (above). Shoppers in London's Oxford Street, 1928 (left).

counters so that ladies could sit while being served with gloves or dress furnishings. Most of the larger stores had tearooms or restaurants where customers were entertained by selections of light music played by a piano trio or quintet. Everything was done to make the experience of visiting the store as pleasant as possible – though it could be rather daunting for those without an account or a fat chequebook.

During the 1930s, window-dressing in department stores became much more sophisticated. Previously, stores had tried to show as many goods as possible in the windows, cramming them on rows and rows of shelves to show how well-stocked they were. Now window-dressers, like interior decorators, had become recognised professionals, and they concentrated on a few well-chosen items, shown against an eye-catching background of scenery and props. This fashion extended also to more specialised shops, such as expensive patisseries or confectioners, which might now show a single (dummy) box of chocolates, strategically and tastefully deployed between a Chinese vase and a piece of fine antique embroidery. Window-dressing was just one aspect of the increasingly sophisticated consumer society.

GERMAN RESENTMENT

However, department stores were not universally popular. In Germany they attracted some degree of hostility from small tradesmen and craftsmen, from whom they were thought to be stealing business. Often Jewish-owned, and regarded as representing mass machine-production, Big Business and international capital, they were viewed by small business owners with resentment. This was just one of the many causes of discontent capitalised upon by Hitler and which helped bring the Nazis to power.

BOY'S WORLD Every little boy's dream: a station for his train set. Christmas shopping in Germany, 1930.

FASHION AND CLOTHING

The most dramatic changes in the history of women's fashions occurred

in the 1920s. Then, in the 1930s, fashion was pulled sometimes

towards glamour, sometimes towards austerity.

DURING the First World War, young women had started to cut their hair shorter, as the long and elaborately dressed hair of the Victorians and Edwardians had become a nuisance for women at work on the farms or in the munitions factories. They were also wearing their skirts shorter, though still well below the knee, and abandoning the stiffly boned corsets that their mothers had worn. They were beginning to wear brassieres, a quite recent invention, rather than camisoles. Some of them had even taken to wearing trousers. In the early 1920s hair began to be cut short in a 'bob', later permanently waved with a 'shingle', and skirts got shorter and shorter. Women began to wear lipstick and nail varnish, something that had previously been considered as very far from respectable.

The years 1926 and 1927 were the classic ones for what we think of as the 'Twenties Look'. Fashionable young women wore their hair in the boyish 'Eton crop'; their skirts, which had lengthened slightly for a brief period in 1922-3, now barely covered the knees; their

A COMPLAINT 'I wish you weren't so modern, mother, it's terribly out of date.' A comment from *Punch* in 1930.

waistlines dropped to the hip; and they cultivated a flat-chested look with 'flatteners'. Hair was held in a bandeau or covered by a cloche hat. This look was particularly the work of the French designer 'Coco' Chanel, whose clothes were strikingly simple and elegant, and whose knitted jackets and jumpers with pleated skirts were widely imitated. Although other

EYEWITNESS

'WE PREFER FLAT NOSES AND CHESTS'

ENGLISH PHOTOGRAPHER Cecil Beaton, writing in *Vogue* magazine in 1928, defends the new look for women – including cropped hair, lipstick, short skirts and even trousers – that is shocking the older generation.

❝ Our standards are so completely changed from the old that comparison or argument is impossible. We can only

say, "But we *like* no chins! Du Maurier's chins are as stodgy as porridge; we *prefer* high foreheads to low ones, we *prefer* flat noses and chests and schoolboy figures to bosoms and hips like watermelons in

AESTHETE
Cecil Beaton, set and costume designer, writer, photographer and artist, in 1932.

season. We like heavy eyelids; they are considered amusing and smart. We adore make-up and the gilded lily, and why not? Small dimpled hands make us feel sick; we like to see the forms of bone and gristle. We flatten our hair on purpose to make it sleek and silky and to show the shape of our skulls, and it is our supreme object to have a head looking like a wet football on a neck as thin as a governess's hatpin." ❞

DRESSMAKING AND KNITTING AT HOME

THE INTRODUCTION of the domestic sewing machine at the turn of the century transformed home dress-making. Even though cheap ready-made clothes were available, women of all classes still had clothes made or modified by the local seamstress, who could work much more quickly, but many made their own clothes at home. The dress patterns available from stores, or provided free by magazines, enabled women to copy even expensive fashion garments and fit them to their own size.

Knitting, however, still had to be done by hand. In the past it had been used only for homely items such as children's jumpers, shawls, gloves,

HOME COUTURE Women who made their own clothes were encouraged by the huge range of patterns available from wool shops, stores and magazines.

comforters or fishermen's sweaters, but from the 1920s on, partly thanks to the influence of Chanel, knitted garments could be high fashion.

Women wore knitted coats and skirts and even knitted hats. Magazines heavily featured knitting patterns, and wool shops opened everywhere.

---

designers such as Paquin, Lanvin, Molyneux and Jean Patou featured heavily in the fashion magazines, it was Chanel who dominated French fashion in the 1920s – and French fashion dominated the Western world. Paris, where in 1918 couture dresses were shown on living models for the first time, was where wealthy and fashionable women the world over went to buy clothes.

The fashion for short skirts was not popular in every quarter. It was denounced by clergymen in both Europe and the United States, the Archbishop of Naples declaring that a recent major earthquake was divine judgment against the shamelessness of the women who wore them. Various American States tried to ban the scandalous fashion for short skirts. A Bill was introduced in Utah in the 1920s to make it a crime to wear 'skirts higher than three inches above the ankle' and another in Ohio banned women over the age of 14 from wearing 'a skirt which does not reach that part of the foot known as the instep'.

AN UPLIFTING IDEA

The modern brassiere was designed in 1914 by the American heiress Caresse Crosby, who spent much of her life in Paris. She may have inherited her inventive gift from her grandfather, Robert Fulton, inventor of the steamship.

To achieve the fashionable tubular look, women became obsessed with slimness and hence with diet and exercise regimes. Wallis Simpson, later the Duchess of Windsor, was quoted at the time as saying 'You can never be too rich or too thin'. This summed up the pressure that women now felt to maintain their looks after marriage. Newspapers and magazines were full of foolproof weight-loss tips – the *Daily Chronicle* in 1927 recommended orange juice with a dash of gin. Chemists sold patent weight-reducers; and gymnasium equipment which rocked the body around to different rhythms enjoyed a vogue, along with rubber rollers designed to massage away superfluous fat. Doctors warned about the dangers of excessive slimming, but the obsession continued until the early 1930s, when fashion allowed women to be more curvaceous again.

Now that young women were showing so much of their legs, stockings became available in a variety of different shades, including flesh-coloured: in silk for those who

POWDER PUFF Fashion demanded powdered knees with rolled-down stockings.

COURTAULDS' FABRICS

CASUAL ELEGANCE
The fashionable Longchamp races provide the excuse to show off a chic 1920s Parisian couture outfit.

TWENTIES STYLE A poster (above) shows a young woman shimmering in petticoat and silk stockings. Mother and daughter (left) model knitwear and cloche hats in Berlin.

summer, women might even leave their stockings off altogether, although the suggestion that they could do so when playing tennis at Wimbledon was viewed as outrageous. Lingerie became much lighter, briefer and more alluring, and when it was advertised as such in the newspapers, it shocked many older people – especially Churchmen.

could afford them and in rayon for the rest. (Rayon production in the USA went from £8 million in 1920 to £53 million in 1925). For informal occasions in the

SUN WORSHIP

By the end of the 1920s swimming costumes exposed the arms and legs, and beach robes and beach pyjamas were beginning to appear. No longer was it fashionable to have a pale complexion; instead, suntans were all the rage. By 1929 suntan oil was available as a beauty product and the more up-market fashion magazines were discreetly recommending readers to sunbathe in

FLAPPER FASHION Casual clothes and rolled-down stockings modelled by Florida bathing beauties on a Columbia Six (above). Kissproof, an American face powder (left) 'lasts longer'.

the nude for an all-over tan. With so much emphasis on outdoor activities specially designed sportswear, particularly in the look created by the fashion designer Worth, was now available.

From 1926 on, hair and skirts began to grow longer again, and after 1929 and the Depression that followed it, fashion changed quite sharply. Hemlines dropped almost overnight in 1929. Two contrary influences were at work. Firstly, it was felt unsmart to look rich when so many were impoverished: clothes became less frivolous; cheaper materials such as cotton were being used, even for couture evening dresses, as Chanel showed in a collection in 1931; and zip-fasteners and press-studs were making clothes easier to make, and simpler to wear. Secondly, Hollywood, now enormously influential, emphasised glamour. What Greta Garbo, Joan Crawford and Katherine Hepburn wore was now at least as influential as what was worn in Paris. Many more women were now using heavy make-up, copying what they could see in close-ups on the screen or in movie magazines. Sales of lipstick and cosmetics soared. (In 1931, 1500 lipsticks were sold in London for every one that had been sold in 1920.)

High fashion in the 1930s was more varied, reflecting the styles of a larger number of designers. Coco Chanel was still popular but her dominant position was challenged by Schiaparelli, who was influenced by the work of the

A GLIMPSE OF STOCKING ... was looked on as something shocking but the motto of the age was 'anything goes'.

AVANT-GARDE A Benito drawing for *Vogue* shows summer fashions. Slacks were still quite daring in 1930.

IN THE SWIM The 1930s saw swimsuits transformed. At the beginning of the decade, swimwear was still one-piece (above); by 1937 it was two-piece, as in the Elizabeth Arden 'Sunpruf Cream' advertisement (left). The bikini did not appear until 1946.

Surrealist painters, and by newer designers such as Balenciaga, who left Spain at the outbreak of the Civil War, and Mainbocher, who dressed the fashion-conscious Duchess of Windsor. As Parisian couture clothes began to seem expensive to many buyers, American and British designers gained more attention. As a result, there was no clear equivalent in the 1930s to the look created for the 1920s by Chanel.

Women now began to emphasise their femininity, rather than trying to look boyish. Under the influence of Hollywood, they started buying rubber girdles and uplift brassieres, both of American design, in order to draw attention to their waists and bosoms. For swimsuits and evening dresses the back was left almost entirely bare. Skirts were drawn tightly across the hips, and shoulders were padded to contrast with the slimness of the waist. Hemlines varied in length according to the occasion and the time of day.

More attention was paid to hats, which became more fanciful than the simple cloche, and to higher-heeled shoes, which were now made in a wide variety of materials from lizard and crocodile to ostrich and walrus. Sunglasses became a fashion accessory, along with deep-peaked eye-shades for driving, tennis and sunbathing. Clothing in general was more elaborate;

there was even a brief Victorian revival, complete with crinolines, leg-of-mutton sleeves, and Victorian hats and jewellery. A woman's day dress that had required only two yards of material in the mid 1920s required five by 1938 but, thanks to the new materials and dress-fastenings, it was also much lighter in weight and simpler to wear.

By the end of the 1930s one distinctively 'Thirties Look' had emerged: padded shoulders; tailored, slightly mannish suits; and hats that looked a little like men's trilbies. Hair was longer again and generally pinned up on the head. This style was fixed by the years of the Second World War, and did not change again until the postwar 'New Look'.

In general, however, it was only the well-to-do who wore high-fashion clothes, and what is shown in the fashion plates of the 1920s and 30s is not what you would have seen on the streets. Older women and the very poor still wore the styles of the early 1900s, but mass production and new cheap materials, particularly rayon, enabled young working-class women for the first time to wear clothes that quite closely resembled

---

SHORT SERVICE

The first Englishwoman to wear shorts on the tennis court was Miss Eileen Bennett at a London party in July 1933. Her shorts were pleated but caused a sensation nevertheless.

CASUAL ELEGANCE Casual clothes for the smart woman of the 1930s: from France (above), and finely tailored, elegant golfwear from Germany (right).

those of the rich, and to buy new and fashionable clothes much more frequently. In the United States in particular, after a heavy duty had been imposed on the importation of couture models in the 1930s, manufacturers started importing Parisian *toiles* (patterns cut out of linen) from which copies could be made for $50, compared with the $2000 price of an original.

In 1919 men could still be seen wearing frock coats and silk hats. A bowler or homburg hat, a black coat and striped trousers were still considered correct dress for professional men and male clerical workers in the 1920s and 30s. But the lounge suit or flannel trousers and jacket steadily began to establish themselves as normal outdoor wear. Plus fours became a familiar sight on the golf course as well as on the grouse

65

A DILEMMA She: 'Why so pensive, Spike?' He: 'I was thinking of a funny costume to wear at the masked ball.' A comment on men's fashions from America.

moor. Trousers, still narrow in the early 1920s, became looser and wider, and there was a brief fashion in the 1920s for the absurdly wide-legged 'Oxford bags'. Pullovers began to replace waistcoats in casual wear (they were the first garment that could be worn interchangeably by both men and women) and the soft-collared shirt took over, at least at weekends, from the

stiff collar that required front and back studs. Neckties were brighter and wider, and could, on occasion, be dispensed with altogether. Younger men took to wearing wristwatches, an invention of the First World War. Spats, still commonly worn in the 1920s, had virtually disappeared by 1939.

Clothing in general became lighter and more colourful, departing from the earlier uniform grey, black and navy-blue. In the hot summer of 1923 British MP John Hodge made history by turning up in the House of Commons wearing a lemon-coloured shantung silk suit, cream socks and a panama hat.

Upper-class men still dressed for dinner in the evening, but the dinner jacket was an acceptable alternative to the full-length tail coat on all but the most formal occasions. The fashion for these increasingly informal male dress styles was led by Edward, Prince of Wales and later Duke of Windsor, and by such well-dressed Americans as Fred Astaire.

As with women, men who were only moderately well-off could now buy ready-made clothing, a fact that George Orwell noticed in Britain in the mid 1930s, although it was even more true in the United States:

'The youth who leaves school at fourteen and gets a blind-alley job is out of work at twenty, probably for life; but for two pounds ten on the hire-purchase he can buy himself a suit which, for a little while

STRANGE BUT TRUE 'Reformwear' in Berlin (left) and 'Oxford bags' (above), originally from England, in Los Angeles.

PRICE 6½ GNS

GOOD CLOTHES NOW COST FAR LESS . . . The double-breasted suit has come strongly into favour recently. And here you see how it is now being worn. The 'drape,' you will notice, is easy, the long lapel is rolled to the bottom button, the material is in the increasingly popular pastel-blue shade. What is, however, more remarkable about this suit, is that you may buy it, ready-tailored by Simpson craftsmen, for 6½ guineas! Ready-to-wear suits in various fabrics from 5 to 8 guineas. Made-to-measure suits from 6 to 12 guineas

SIMPSON 202 PICCADILLY, REGENT 2002 { There are good men's shops throughout the British Isles who are appointed agents for Simpson tailoring. We will gladly send you the address of the one nearest to you.

THIRTIES MENSWEAR **Plus fours (above) were ideal for walking and bicycling. The suit from Simpson in Piccadilly (left) could be bought for less than £7 and would never be worn without a hat.**

and at a little distance, looks as though it had been tailored in Savile Row. The girl can look like a fashion plate at an even lower price.' But class badges still showed themselves in male dress, not so much in the United States and the Commonwealth countries, but certainly in Europe, and perhaps especially in Britain, where working-class men almost invariably wore cloth caps, and mufflers instead of ties. To wear a hat was still a mark of belonging at least to the lower rungs of the middle class.

Men of all classes still rarely went out without a hat or cap, but the soft felt hat – a trilby or 'porkpie' in Britain, a snap-brimmed hat in America – became increasingly common. Straw boaters, normal summer wear throughout the period in the United States, gradually faded out of use during the 1930s.

Beards, still quite common in 1918, had almost disappeared by 1938. Men were now clean-shaven or wore neatly trimmed moustaches of the type favoured by the film actors Ronald Colman, William Powell and Clark Gable. Hair was worn short, neatly parted, and often smoothed down with brilliantine.

A well-dressed man of the year 1938 would have not looked greatly out of place in the smarter streets of today's cities. On the other hand, a time-traveller from the interwar years would be deeply shocked by the casualness of most younger people's dress today.

MIND YOUR ZIPPER

A zip-fastener was exhibited at the Chicago Exposition of 1893, but the modern zip was not patented until 1913. Its inventor was a Swedish-born engineer from Hoboken, New Jersey, named Gideon Sundback. The Talon Slide Fastener, as it was called, began to take off when the US armed services adopted it for use on flying clothes and other uniforms. After the war it found its way onto leather goods, boots and sports clothes. The British did not take to the zip until 1924, when a giant zipper was exhibited at the Wembley Empire Exhibition and the public were invited to try it for themselves. The first couturier to use zips on women's clothes was Schiaparelli in 1930, but they did not appear on men's trousers until 1935.

FOOD AND DRINK

People could enjoy a wider range of foodstuffs than ever before.

More and more foods were being branded and packaged.

But there were still worries about inadequate diet among the poor.

PROGRESSIVE employers were increasingly providing works canteens in the 1920s and 30s. These became more and more necessary as people worked further from their homes, but many working people and schoolchildren still went home for their midday meal. Breakfast, lunch and, especially, the evening meal were important family rituals, with all the family present at the table.

Food in continental Europe was even more strongly regional in character than today, with people using traditional recipes and local produce as far as possible. Only the markets of the great cities, such as Paris, were full of the produce of the whole country, and of other countries as well.

Britain, with its heavily urbanised population, relied on large quantities of imported food, especially chilled or frozen meat from Argentina, Australia and New Zealand, as well as grain from North America and butter and cheese from New Zealand. In the early 1920s the British depended for fruit mainly on their native apples, pears and plums, with oranges imported for Christmas, but by the end of the interwar years they were familiar with imported tropical fruits such as bananas and even mangoes. Exotic vegetables such as peppers, courgettes or aubergines were rarely to be seen, however. Eating habits in Britain, the United States and the Commonwealth countries remained deeply conservative; all but the very poor or the nutritionally conscious rich expected a substantial dish of meat, potatoes and vegetables at least once a day and most were suspicious of 'foreign' food.

In the Anglo-Saxon countries the wealthier classes were eating on a less lavish scale. The seemingly endless Victorian dinners had been replaced on most occasions by only three or four courses, and North Americans led the way in favouring lighter meals, with salads in place of boiled vegetables, and fruit instead of heavy puddings. Even at a grand occasion such as the

THE FAMILY AT TABLE   In the United States in the 1930s, people were being encouraged to eat a healthier diet.

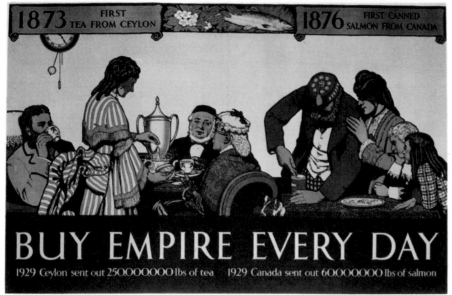

1873 FIRST TEA FROM CEYLON   1876 FIRST CANNED SALMON FROM CANADA

BUY EMPIRE EVERY DAY

1929 Ceylon sent out 250000000 lbs of tea   1929 Canada sent out 60000000 lbs of salmon

IMPERIAL CONNECTIONS One of many posters for the Empire Marketing Board, founded in the 1920s to encourage British people to buy Empire produce.

the poorer social classes partly because of their heavy use of cheap jams and syrups and the quantity that went into endless cups of tea.' These, together with white bread, margarine and an occasional kipper, were the hallmarks of the poverty-line diet that George Orwell observed in *The Road to Wigan Pier*.

The diet of working people was not always so grim, however. Here is the wife of an East End docker, earning just over £2 per week in the 1930s (she was a Catholic, who did not eat meat on Fridays):

'I find it all right to give them minced meat on Mondays for their dinner, and gravy on Tuesdays. Wednesdays we have just a small meat pudding; Thursdays, a baked dinner with lamb chops and baked potatoes and cabbage and Yorkshire pudding. Friday is a day of fish, which depends on which is the best to be had. On Saturday we usually have braised steak and potatoes and cabbage, or else we have liver and bacon. On Sunday I have only a small piece of meat, such as a piece of beef or small half-shoulder of lamb, with baked potatoes, Yorkshire or suet pudding, with cabbage or greens that are in season . . . My husband, if at work, is at home at 5 o'clock in the evening, and then there is his tea. Monday, usually eggs and bacon; Tuesday, lamb chops; Wednesday, steak and onions; Thursday may be ham or a little meat left from dinner, and Friday he eats nothing but fish or eggs and cheese.'

THE DEMON DRINK

Drinking habits were strongly national. Continental Europeans drank wine, beer or cider according to their region – in 1926, the average per

wedding breakfast of the Duke and Duchess of York (the future King George VI and Queen Elizabeth) in 1923, there were a mere eight courses – less than half the number that would have been served before the war.

The North Americans and the British still had their traditional regional dishes but they were increasingly using packaged, tinned and, from the early 1930s, frozen food, and relying generally on their large national food-manufacturing industries. Knowledge of scientific nutrition – especially the importance of vitamins and of balancing proteins, fats and carbohydrates – increased during the period. But at the same time the diet of many people probably became unhealthier, partly due to the poverty associated with unemployment, and partly because of the increasingly popular use of processed convenience foods. The historian John Burnett writes of Britain in the 1930s:

'A nutritionally adequate diet was probably possible in the 1930s for five-sixths of the population, but because of ignorance or prejudice, lack of time or lack of facilities, only half the population was able to receive it . . . Sugar consumption was so high in

POPCORN The contents of the box were emptied into the popcorn machine.

CONSUMER CHOICE An attentive shop assistant helps with the choice of fruit.

capita consumption in France was 136 litres, mainly of wine – and their own national aperitifs, spirits and liqueurs. In Britain, the United States and Canada only the well-to-do drank wine regularly (the Australian wine industry was just beginning to develop). Working-class men drank beer; but a large proportion of the population rarely, if ever, drank alcohol. In the 1930s there was a successful bid to open milk bars as a non-alcoholic alternative to pubs and bars. The British as a whole were drinking less, partly because of the restrictive licensing laws introduced during the First World War, but partly because there were more alternatives to drinking in public houses; tea was now the national drink. The Bright Young Things, though, had taken to the American habit of drinking cocktails before dinner, instead of the more traditional sherry or whisky-and-soda. They were also drinking in night-clubs and at the fashionable 'bottle parties'. As the working class became more sober, a section of the upper class was getting drunker, to an extent that would have shocked its grandparents' generation.

PROHIBITION

From 1920 to 1933 the United States had the Prohibition, a law which banned the sale and consumption of alcohol. But Americans continued to drink in speakeasies and to consume illicit homemade corn whiskey or the liquor supplied by the 'bootleggers'. (The output of corn sugar, whose main use was the manufacture of liquor, went up six-fold between 1919 and 1929.) They could also drink wine that had been stored in their own cellars before the Eighteenth Amendment went into effect in January 1920, or make their own from grape juice. It is not certain that Americans as a whole drank more during the Prohibition years; certainly, many who had been moderate or non-drinkers, and especially women, took to drinking spirits from hip-flasks or frequenting speakeasies from 1920 onwards.

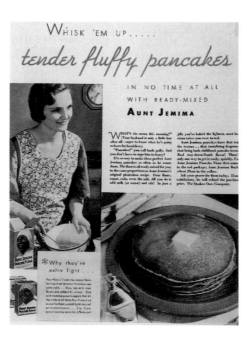

FAST FOOD It was not exactly home cooking, but ready-mixed foods, like these American pancakes, were easy to make and saved time.

Continental Europeans had long been accustomed to eating out regularly in inexpensive neighbourhood restaurants – there were 10 000 of these in Paris alone in the 1930s – especially for Sunday lunch. In the Anglo-Saxon world, eating out was still, for most people, an occasional treat. But the British now had Lyons' Corner Houses, in which inexpensive meals were served in quite grand surroundings by 'nippies' (waitresses smartly dressed in black dresses with caps and aprons) or similarly inexpensive restaurants in cinemas and department stores. Americans were getting used to fast-food in the diners, with their 'modernistic' fittings in shiny chrome, or in the new automats, with self-service from specially designed cabinets. Grand restaurants in the Anglo-Saxon world were almost entirely French; moderately priced ones Italian, or occasionally Greek or German. More exotic foods, Chinese or Indian for example, could be found only near ports or in immigrant areas; going to eating places of that kind was thought to be quite adventurous. But for special occasions and festivities, such as Thanksgiving or Christmas, the family table at home was still the right place to be.

SHOPS AND SUPERMARKETS

The first 'supermarkets' (the Alpha Beta Food Market in Pomona, Ward's Grocetaria in Ocean Park and the 'Humpty Dumpty Stores' chain) had opened in California in 1912 and large-scale grocery stores such as the King Kullen chain began to appear in other parts of the United States in the 1930s. But elsewhere they were unknown

TOUJOURS PARIS The stylish French café-brasserie looks now much as it did then.
The *Gitanes* cigarette pack (right) was designed by M. Ponty and appeared in 1930.

until the 1950s. People still did their local shopping in open street markets or in specialist local shops: the butcher, the baker, the fishmonger and the grocer. Those who had telephones could use them to order their meat or groceries, which were then delivered, either by a boy on a specially designed bicycle or, increasingly, by light vans.

Chainstores such as the Great Atlantic & Pacific Tea Company in the United States and Sainsbury, Dewhurst, W.H. Smith and Marks and Spencer in Britain, were becoming a familiar feature; in continental Europe they were, as yet, largely unknown. The American-owned Woolworth, whose British slogan was 'nothing over sixpence', was a household name. It sold a huge variety of goods,

UNIFORM SERVICE At Lyons' chain of Corner House restaurants in England, the waitresses were referred to, somewhat unflatteringly, as 'nippies'.

from kitchen utensils and household linen to cosmetics and jewellery, at low prices that forced other shops in the neighbourhood to reduce theirs, and though it catered mainly for the working class, the well-to-do also found its bargains attractive.

Grocers would still weigh out some goods from bulk supplies kept in sacks behind the counter and wrap them up in neat brown paper packages, but many branded goods, including many of those familiar today such as Heinz, Campbell, Nestlé and Kelloggs, were available. Eggs, milk and butter were graded and guaranteed fresh, and even oranges and bananas were branded. Branded American breakfast cereals which needed only the addition of milk were steadily gaining ground over Britain's traditional porridge, which in any case could now be cooked much more quickly in the form of Quick Quaker Oats. Convenience foods were

71

becoming increasingly popular, and before the end of the 1930s virtually every kind of meat, fish, fruit and vegetable could be bought in cans or bottles, and the first frozen foods, marketed by Clarence Birdseye, were appearing on the shelves. Hygiene in food shops was generally improving: butchers had begun storing their carcasses in refrigerators, and by the 1930s Cellophane was helping to keep food fresh and clean.

THE AGE OF ADVERTISING

Sales of branded goods were strongly supported by advertising – in the Press, on hoardings and on the radio – which was now a familiar feature of every-day life and a rapidly growing industry. In the United States alone, the amount of advertising done in 1927 cost over a billion and a half dollars. Advertising

GOOD FOR YOU
Much emphasis was put on nutrition and diet. Advertisers tried to make even chocolate appear 'healthy'.

CAPTAIN BIRDSEYE

The first individually packaged frozen food products were put on sale by Clarence Birdseye in Springfield, Massachusetts, in 1930. While on a trip to Labrador, Birdseye noticed that fish froze instantly when taken out of the water in sub-zero temperatures but that months later, when thawed, some of them were still alive. By 1933 there were over 500 frozen-food outlets in the USA. Frozen foods, including asparagus, strawberries, garden peas, raspberries and green beans, first appeared in Britain in 1937, marketed by Smedley.

had played a major part in the struggle to match mass consumption with mass production. The fact that demand never quite caught up with the supply of goods was one of the major contributory factors leading to the Depression of the 1930s.

Advertisements promised relief from ailments, or effective hygiene – Listerine reduced germs 'up to 86.7 per cent' – or played on anxiety about bad breath, body odour or such recently discovered concerns as 'night starvation', 'five o'clock shadow' or 'dated skin'. Cigarette advertisements announced that their products were harmless – 'Not a cough in a carload' – or positively beneficial – 'Camels give digestion a helping hand'. When the American Tobacco Company used the slogan 'Reach for a Lucky instead of a sweet' US sweet manufacturers united to take newspaper advertisements to combat any potential fall in sweet sales. Cigarette smoking had increased greatly since the First World

HIGH STREET SHOPPING The high street in Letchworth, England. Note the delivery boy and the absence of motor cars.

FOOD AND DRINK ADVERTISING BETWEEN THE WARS

COMMERCIAL ART flourished in the interwar years and, together with advances in printing, it became more colourful and sophisticated. Huge sums were spent on campaigns to launch new products or maintain brand loyalty. Many commercial artists were influenced by the avant-garde art of the day, and people grew accustomed to modernist features in advertisements, as in the Nestlé ad below. Advertisers saw the advantage of the constantly repeated slogan, such as 'Guinness is good for you', and the Coca-Cola Company led the way in identifying its products with an entire lifestyle and making its product logo recognised worldwide.

Is that my GUINNESS?

GUINNESS GETS HOME

THIRST APPEAL Guinness advertising was lighthearted, and Bateman's drawings, usually directed at British institutions, were hugely popular.

SODA FOUNTAIN A Coca-Cola ad (right) from about 1925.

CHOC-FULL OF GOODNESS !

Drink Coca-Cola
Delicious and Refreshing

The Coca-Cola Company, Atlanta, Ga.

AT A COOL AND CHEERFUL PLACE
You'll find a wonderful girl in a real American pose – at the soda fountain — When thirsty remember her.

RE-FRESH YOURSELF. FIVE CENTS IS THE PRICE

CHILD APPEAL A British poster for Nestlé (above) appeared in 1929.

BEDTIME DRINK A traditional malted coffee drink from Germany (right) is restyled for the 1930s.

Kathreiners Malz-kaffee

JAMBON VILLETTE
CELUI DE LA PRÉSIDENCE

BEST HAM An illustration by Jean d'Ylen for Villette ham. Their slogan was 'as used by the Presidency'.

COMMERCIAL ART The poster had its heyday in the years between the wars. This classic design for Sandeman Port appeared all over Europe.

an organisation that conquered the world . . . Nowhere is there such a startling example of executive success as the way in which that organisation was brought together.'

In the course of the interwar years the advertisers' output became more sophisticated; on the visual side, it was increasingly influenced by avant-garde art and graphic design. Advertisements were also becoming subtler, paying less attention to the product's qualities and more to the hopes and fears they strove to associate with it: to people's cravings to be young and desirable or to have a home that neighbours would envy, to their terror of being shunned for bad breath or looked down upon for having inadequate social skills. Until the Crash came, advertising was one of the main driving forces behind the remarkable prosperity of the United States.

JUNK FOOD

Altogether, working people had the chance to buy a wider range of foodstuffs – and hence the possibility of a healthier diet – than ever before, although concern was already being expressed about the increased consumption of 'junk food', especially now that products such as heavily processed white bread, potato crisps and instant

War, especially among women, who considered it modern and stylish. In Britain 80 per cent of men and 40 per cent of women smoked, and the figures were similar elsewhere.

Advertising executives became influential members of society. An American nonfiction bestseller of the 1920s, Bruce Barton's *The Man Nobody Knows,* claimed that if Jesus Christ had been alive then he would have been an account executive in an advertising agency – 'He picked up twelve men from the bottom ranks of business and forged them into

coffee were available. Their new spending power was not always welcomed in other respects either. George Orwell noted, rather sourly:

'Whole sections of the working class who have been plundered of all they really need are being compensated, in part, by cheap luxuries which mitigate the surface of life . . . It is quite likely that fish-and-chips, art-silk stockings, tinned salmon, cut-price chocolate . . . the movies, the radio, strong tea and the football pools have between them averted revolution.'

It is not clear what he felt they really needed.

WORK AND PLAY BETWEEN THE WARS

New industries were springing up in the 1920s and 30s,

offering unheard-of prosperity. But mass production could

mean demeaning, repetitive work, and finding a job at all became

a problem in the Depression years. Meanwhile, there was

an abundance of new leisure opportunities for

those who could afford them.

WORK, WEALTH AND WAGES

There was still a wide gap between rich and poor.

But now gaps were opening up between those who had work

and those who did not.

DURING the 1920s and 30s, the types of work people did changed and the workplace was transformed. It was electrified. All over the developed world vast numbers of giant poles were erected to carry electrical power supplies to homes and factories, disfiguring the countryside as they strode across the landscape. Some modernist contemporary poets and artists saw these as a symbol of the exciting future that science and technology would bring, ultimately freeing people from the tyranny of labour; others, with a more traditional perspective, deplored them as examples of the ugliness of the modern industrial world. But whatever effect it had on the landscape, electrical power freed the newer industries from a dependence on the coalfields. It brought

manufacturing work to entirely new areas where the factories, springing up on what had for centuries been agricultural land, were cleaner and less polluting.

As well as transforming the workplace, electricity heralded the age of the cinema, broadcasting and suburban electric trains – and the first wave of electrical domestic appliances. (The spread of electricity was seen as so important in the new Soviet Russia that many babies were named Electra – a derivative of the Russian word for 'electrification'.)

Industry became more and more mechanised. In the German mining industry, for example, more than 90 per cent of coal had been extracted manually in 1913; by 1929 nearly all of it was being extracted by using electrically powered tools and transported

---

EYEWITNESS

KEEPING UP APPEARANCES

THE DEPRESSION struck at all classes. George Orwell believed that when middle-class people were reduced to living on meagre incomes they suffered more than the working class, because of their need to keep up middle-class appearances. In his semi-autobiographical novel *Keep the Aspidistra Flying*, he gave a tragicomic description of what that meant:

❢ It had taken him an hour or more to get himself ready. Social life is so complicated when your income is two quid a week. He had had a painful shave in cold water immediately before dinner. He had put on his best suit; three years old but just passable when he remembered to press the

trousers under his mattress. He had turned his collar inside out and tied his tie so that the torn place didn't show. With the point of a match he had scraped enough blacking from the tin to polish his shoes. He had even borrowed a needle from Lorenheim and darned his socks – a tedious job, but better than inking the places where your ankle shows through. Also he had procured an empty Gold Flake packet and put into it a single cigarette extracted from the penny-in-the-slot machine. That was just for the look of the thing. You can't, of course, go to other people's houses with no cigarettes. But if you have even one it's all right, because

when people see one cigarette in a packet they assume that the packet has been full. It is fairly easy to pass the thing off as an accident.

"Have a cigarette?" you say casually to someone.

"Oh! thanks."

You push the packet open and then register surprise. 'Hell! I'm down to my last. And I could have sworn I had a full packet."

"Oh, I won't take your last. Have one of mine." says the other.

"Oh! thanks."

And after that, of course, your host and hostess press cigarettes upon you. But you must have one cigarette, just for honour's sake. ❢

PERSPECTIVES OF INDUSTRY   The coal mines of Duisburg (above) were typical of the industrial landscape of the Ruhr, Germany, in the 1930s. Car assembly lines at Renault, France (right), stretch seemingly to the horizon.

through the mine on mechanised conveyor belts. In mines everywhere, individual output rose enormously – although the numbers of men employed also dropped sharply; more than half of all German miners were unemployed in the Depression of the 1930s and there was similar distress in mining areas throughout Europe and North America. Although baths were introduced in many mines for the workers to use after coming up from the pit, in the 1930s, mining was still dirty – and dangerous – work.

At the same time, because work was being organised in a more sophisticated way, and because of the sheer range and variety of things now being produced and marketed, there was a vast increase in the demand for workers in 'white-collar' technical, administrative and clerical jobs, and many more people began to be employed in what is now known as the 'services' sector, for example in new and rapidly growing areas such as advertising and public relations.

Traditional heavy industries began to give way to newer ones: pharmaceuticals; packaging (demand for which had increased with the development of branded goods); electrical goods; auto-mobile production (which trebled in the course of the 1920s); the manufacture of synthetic materials such as Bakelite and synthetic rubber and synthetic textiles such as rayon; and, right at the end of the 1930s, nylon.

These changes were very localised. In every country there were traditional industrial areas, such as Pennsylvania or the Ruhr or the North of England, where there were still Victorian factories and working conditions, low wages and, in the 1930s, high unemployment; and new areas, such as California or the South-east of England, with bright new factories, high wages and high employment. It was as if part of the population

NEW MATERIAL   Bakelite, a synthetic resin, appeared and was moulded to form small household products and packages like this dentifrice container of about 1930.

A Modern Factory in 1928

Writing in *A History of Everyday Things in England*, Marjorie and C.H.B. Quennell describe a visit to part of the Ford Automobile Factory at Dearborn, Michigan:

❝ We saw it when we were at Dearborn in 1928 and it is the finest industrial interior we have ever seen. The construction is in concrete and steel, and all the upper part is painted. The

MASS PRODUCTION The moving assembly line used by the Ford Motor Company revolutionised industrial production.

whole of the floor is covered with polished maple. In front of each machine is a rubber mat, and a neat cabinet for the tools. The machinery is driven by motors, and there are no unsightly pulleys and shafting. All cables are in a base-

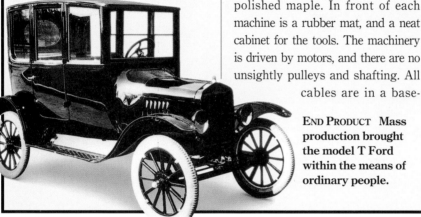

END PRODUCT Mass production brought the model T Ford within the means of ordinary people.

ment. We remember in one of the bays a large printing press with plenty of space around it so that it could be seen, and kept all glittering and bright like the inside of a watch. It was really a beautiful sight. All the lavatories were in the basement, and these would not have disgraced a West-End club in London. That is one very good point about American factories, the sanitary accommodation is always excellent. That filthy thing the round towel is never used. An American employer once tried to introduce it but he was taken outside and hanged from a tree with it, which discouraged others from following suit. Generally a paper towel is used, and then thrown into a basket. In some places you press a knob and dry your hands over a hot-air blast. ❞

was living in the 20th century while others still lived in the 19th. In the traditional areas there were still 'dark, satanic mills', some of them still steam-driven. There were still iron foundries where men sweated so much in the heat and glare that they needed to drink many pints of beer at the end of the day just to restore lost body fluid. There were still textile mills where the noise of the looms was so loud that workers had to learn to lip-read in order to communicate with each other. In some areas there were still 'knockers-up' who walked around the streets in the early morning, rousing men and women without clocks to prepare themselves for work. The factory hooter still sounded through the town at the beginning and end of the working day, summoning crowds of cloth-capped men to pass through the factory gates.

There were still mining disasters – one of the worst examples in Britain was the explosion in 1934 at Gresford Colliery, near Wrexham, on the border of England and Wales, in which 264 men were killed.

And there were still frequent industrial injuries and fatalities from, for example, using heavy machines running without safety guards. Indeed, for example, in Britain the number of fatal accidents between the wars was almost twice what it was in the 1960s, when the workforce was larger.

Yet in other parts of the country there were 'clean' factories in the pharmaceutical or electrical goods industries, where rows of shining machines were tended by lines of workers in crisp clean uniforms. These workers – often young women doing jobs that required very little training – could enjoy company leisure facilities, medical services and subsidised canteens, all supervised by personnel officers.

However, as the unemployment figures continued to rise during the 1930s, men who had served long apprenticeships but who now found themselves out of work looked with bewilderment, and sometimes resentment, at these women who, it seemed to them, had stolen their livelihoods.

Victorian factories had grown haphazardly, occupying an assortment of premises not unlike large domestic buildings. The new factories, however, were specifically built and designed for whatever process went on in them – a type of building that had never been seen before.

In major industries, such as engineering, chemicals and motor manufacture, factories became immensely large, and occupied whole areas of towns and cities, like the huge Renault plant in France, General Motors in Detroit or the Krupps works in Germany.

TIME AND MOTION **A worker's movements are filmed through a grid in a study aimed at eliminating 'wasted time and motion'.**

SEGREGATION OF WORK AND HOME

The introduction of zoning regulations segregated industrial and residential areas, destroying the old mixed neighbourhoods in which factories had jostled side-by-side with houses, shops and small businesses. As a result, people often lived farther from where they worked and increasingly they travelled to work by public transport, by bicycle, or, in North America, by car. The workplace and the home became more separate than they had ever been.

Work in the larger factories was becoming organised on the principles instituted by Henry Ford in the United States. Products and product parts were standardised as far as possible, and the process of manufacturing them broken down into its individual components. Parts were made by specialised machine tools and then fitted together on a moving assembly line. Workers were no longer required to be craftsmen responsible for products in their entirety; instead, they came to be regarded as units of labour, each with his own place on the assembly line and his own very specific task to perform. Whereas a skilled fitter had to take a seven-year apprenticeship to master his trade, his successor on the assembly line could learn the work required of him in seven hours. Workers were seen as parts of a highly efficient machine. At the same time, the 'scientific management' techniques developed by the American engineer Frederic Taylor

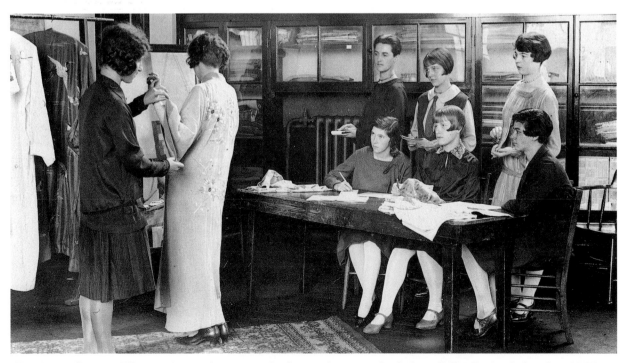

THE ART OF SELLING **Women shop assistants receive instruction at a school of retail distribution in London, 1927.**

(1856-1915) included 'time-and-motion' studies, in which the workers' movements were observed, timed and restructured for optimum efficiency. These techniques increased output and reduced labour costs, thus making possible the mass production of inexpensive consumer goods that was the basis of the new mass prosperity of the 1920s.

But there was a negative side to these new techniques. The work could be dehumanising. Although Henry Ford was in many ways a progressive employer, Taylorism and Fordism took no account of the private needs and goals of the worker or of his feelings as a social being. In his film *Modern Times,* Charlie Chaplin plays an assembly line worker performing a single repetitive operation with his hands. When the whistle blows for a coffee break, his hands keep making the movements they have been making for the past two or three hours; consequently he can't stop them long enough to hold a cup and can only manage to grab a glass of water before work resumes. (Assembly line workers who saw the film did not find this scene funny: it was too near the truth of their own experience.)

From first-hand experience the British writer Walter Greenwood described what assembly line work was like at the Ford works at Trafford Park, Manchester, in the late 1920s:

'When an employee of the Motor Works passed through the works' gates to the clocking-on machines he stepped from Britain into Detroit where Moloch, in the shape of the Main Line Assembly, held unrelenting sway. Parallel tracks down the central aisles of the main shop's length crept forward at a preset pace. Tributary feeder tracks at angles conveniently placed and moving at synchronised speed delivered the prefabricated bits and pieces to the servitors who had to be at their stations along the lines the moment the klaxon blared its imperious and ear-lacerating dissonance. And there the workers stayed, each performing his repetitive operation, until the hooter screamed again signalling the half-hour midday break and the mad rush into the street, rain or shine, to bolt a boxed lunch and devour a cigarette before the siren's discord recalled the hirelings to the paralysing monotony of the endless afternoon.'

This dehumanising process was made even worse, particularly in the United States, by the cruelty of the 'speed-up', in which the time allotted to a specific task was progressively reduced and wages docked from any worker who failed to stick to it. Workers who were subject to the 'speed-up' complained that it left them too exhausted at the end of the working day to do anything but sleep.

PATERNAL EMPLOYERS

Many owners, of even the largest companies, were still private individuals rather than corporate shareholders. They could be seen on the factory floor, and knew the names of at least their longer-serving employees. The attitude of many such owners was still paternalistic: the smaller ones would give presents to employees when their children were born and preference to their sons and daughters when vacancies arose; the larger provided medical benefits, bonuses, sports clubs and outings. As a result, many were shocked and indignant when, as increasingly

INDUSTRIAL TOWNSCAPE
Lancashire cotton mills in 1925 (above). Steam and electric power are both in use.

ELECTRIC POWER
American engineers (left) pose on a huge electric motor destined to propel a ship.

A COG IN THE WHEEL Charlie Chaplin's *Modern Times* reflected the monotonous nightmare of production-line work.

happened in the 1920s and 30s, the state or the trades unions attempted to intervene in industrial relations; this was seen as gross intrusion into private property and personal relations.

By no means all manual workers were employed in factories. Although many more people worked away from their homes than before the First World War, there were still, for example, over 350 000 home-based workers in France in the late 1930s. Some of these were self-employed craftsmen, but the majority were outworkers, doing work and charging by the piece for factories or merchants. Many were recent immigrants, and the majority were probably women. These outworkers laboured in their cramped homes from dawn to dusk trying to make a living as weavers, seamstresses, glovemakers or shoemakers, unprotected either by trade unions or by the sickness and unemployment benefits that were beginning to be paid to factory workers.

In Germany in the late 1920s, more than one-third of people in employment worked as shopkeepers, craftsmen, farm labourers or were helping in small family businesses. But the trend everywhere was moving away from home employment and into paid employment in industry. In Germany, for example,

between 1905 and 1927 the proportion of female domestic servants dropped from 16 per cent to 11 per cent, and of agricultural workers from 15 per cent to 10 per cent, while the percentage of those employed as industrial workers rose proportionately. At the lowest end of the employment scale were the sweatshops in the garment industry, some of the worst of which were to be found in the United States. In New York

GOOD EXAMPLE Employers with vision cared for their workers. This is an English village fête for Cadbury employees and their families.

THE DEPRESSION IN AUSTRALIA

PATSY ADAM-SMITH was a child when the Depression struck Australia: She describes the lot of the unemployed in *Beyond the Dreamtime*:

❛ Soup queues and handouts were poor compensation for men who'd driven trains across a wilderness, travelled the great shearing routes of the outback, boasted of their strength and endurance and been proud of their day's toil. "What does 'redundant' mean?" a man asked Dad. "They say there's nothing wrong with my work, but I'm not to turn up on Monday because I'm redundant." Looking out of the train windows as we rattled through the inner suburbs, staring down into their mean little back yards, Mum once said, "I wonder what's behind those back doors. Some poor woman, I imagine. God help her."

We knew it wasn't only the labouring classes who were suffering: professional men knocked on our door asking for work. Dad was now a ganger and every man wanted a job in his gang. Shopkeepers, businessmen, farmers – all were in distress. In 1930 those still in work were victims of the emergency reduction of the basic wage. It brought my father's pay down to £2 17s 6d a week. "Oh," people say today, "but you could buy much more with that in those days." You could not. It had been designed as enough for a family to survive on – nothing more. For most of the Depression we lived "Beyond the black stump", that imaginary line where one is out of reach of succour, out in the space where one has only one's own resources and courage to fall back on! ❜

GENERAL STRIKE During the British General Strike of 1926 armoured cars patrolled the London streets to maintain law and order.

City, where 50 000 women were employed in the garment industry, hat-makers crocheted hats for 40 cents a dozen and apron girls were paid two-and-a-half cents an apron; they had to work hard to earn one dollar a week.

The demand for labour during the First World War had strengthened the hand of the Trade Union movement. In the countries of Western Europe, trade unions and the right of collective bargaining had been legalised by the 1920s, and governments had passed laws to introduce shorter working hours – the eight-hour day was widespread – safety at work measures, sickness and unemployment benefits and paid holidays. Weimar Germany was particularly advanced in such legislation, although, due to desperate economic conditions, the state was least able to deliver welfare benefits when most needed. But trade union membership everywhere increased, and the 1920s in particular were characterised by frequent strikes, which from time to time erupted into violence when feelings ran high, as in the British General Strike of 1926, when workers attacked buses driven by undergraduate 'scabs' and the Army was brought in to help run essential services and to stand by in case of any severe breakdown in civil order. But in Europe, although the police, generally speaking, sided with the Establishment, and there were baton charges on demonstrating strikers from time to time, there was far more bloodshed between political factions than there was in industrial disputes.

INDUSTRIAL VIOLENCE

In the United States the situation was rather different. Intellectually and emotionally, Americans were opposed to the notion of state intervention in industrial relations, or of state welfare. Immediately after the Bolshevik Revolution in Russia, there had been a 'Red Scare' in the United States which led employers, and indeed many ordinary citizens, to regard even moderate demands for higher wages or improved conditions as a Bolshevik threat to private property and 'the American way'. Hence, while some employers introduced 'welfare capitalism' in the form of profit-sharing or recreational facilities, attempts to take

SPILT MILK 1935, and striking dairy workers in Ohio push over a milk truck belonging to their employer.

industrial action through strikes or 'sit-ins' were resisted, often violently. Organisers of industrial unions were murdered and strikers were beaten up or shot by armed 'company' police. The Democratic governor of Georgia, Eugene Talmadge, built a detention camp for picketers, and other governors regularly called out the National Guard to suppress unruly workers. The Pittsburg Coal Company kept machine guns trained on the men working in its pits; when asked why by a congressional committee, the Chairman replied, 'You cannot run the mines without them.' Mine owners in Duquesne, Pennsylvania, bombed the homes of miners suspected of planning to organise strikes and burned crosses on hillsides. In the same state, the district attorney in Johnstown declared: 'Give me two hundred good, tough armed men and I'll clean up them sons-of-bitches on the picket line.'

Referring to industrial unrest in the sweatshops of the garment industry, the trade journal *Fibre and Fabric* declared: 'A few hundred funerals will have a quieting influence.'

Local police in the company towns regularly sided with the employers – in Minneapolis in 1934 they shot into an unarmed crowd, killing two and wounding more than 60 others. In Chicago in 1937, 500 armed police attacked a crowd of strikers and their families, killing ten and wounding more than 90. When the federal authorities protested, the company towns replied that as they were privately owned Washington could have no authority over them. Many claimed that the strikers were subversive Communists, bent on infiltrating the towns to cause havoc.

Referring to the 1930s, a

STRONG ARM OF THE LAW
A man demonstrating against unemployment in 1936 is forcibly led away.

83

Presidential Commission on Violence in 1969 stated that the United States 'has had the bloodiest and most violent labor history of any industrial nation in the world'. This was true. Although there were clashes with the police in Europe, unions there were recognised by the state (only until 1933 in the case of Germany), and strikes were on the whole settled by negotiation, or, at worst, by attrition. The striking British miners of 1926 might be brought to near-starvation, but they were not attacked with firearms. The British Hunger Marches of the 1930s were relatively peaceful affairs. The best known of them, the 1936 march from the northern shipbuilding town of Jarrow, where some seven out of ten people were unemployed, was small, apolitical and peaceful. The sight of the pale, thin, poorly clothed men marching quietly in their broken shoes or boots won immense sympathy from people previously inclined to believe that Hunger Marches were a charade organised by subversive Communists. Other marches were larger, and sometimes more violent, but it was more typical of British unemployed workers to lie down in front of the traffic in London's Oxford Street and be politely removed by police, or to invade the Ritz Hotel and ask for tea, as they did in 1938, than to engage in attacks on property or be violently attacked themselves.

Only a passionately held belief in the sacredness of private property, and an almost religious conviction that any organised union activity was a Bolshevik threat to the American way of life, could explain the savage character of industrial relations in the United States in the 1930s.

However, against this background, the material welfare of industrial workers in the more progressive parts of the economy steadily increased in the interwar years. The great gulf was not only between rich and poor, but between, on the one hand, those employed in the advancing sectors of the economy, and, on the

PUBLIC ENEMY The bank robber John Dillinger with Tommy gun; a photograph taken just before he was killed in 1934.

other, the unemployed and those employed in depressed parts of the economy. When, in the 1930s, bank robbers such as John Dillinger and the notorious partners-in-crime Bonnie Parker and Clyde Barrow took to the road many regarded them as modern-day Robin Hoods.

This was one of the cruel paradoxes of the inter-war years. Throughout the industrial world, there were areas which enjoyed increasing prosperity and others which suffered 70 per cent or higher levels of unemployment, with all the attendant misery. The hunger marchers from the North of England who came to London in the 1930s were seen gazing with astonishment at the signs of wealth they saw around them, as if they had come from a different planet.

ON THE LAND

Agriculture, which had thrived during the First World War, fell into a deep depression in the 1920s, due mainly to the huge surpluses that had accumulated in the war years. In the United States, where 25 per cent of the population still lived on the land, the Crash of 1929 made an already desperate situation even worse. Prices fell to their lowest level since the 16th century. Farmers were getting less than 25 cents for a bushel of wheat (which had fetched $1.50 in the war years), five cents for a pound of cotton or wool, two and a half cents for a pound of pork or beef; and yet there were millions of town-dwellers who could not afford to pay even these prices. A small farmer, paying mortgage interest on his land, could lose money on every acre he reaped. It made better economic sense to burn corn than to sell it and buy coal. One Montana rancher shot all his cattle because the price they would fetch was not worth the cost of feeding them.

With prices so low, farmers were unable to keep up payments on their mortgages; the banks foreclosed on thousands of farms, forcing their former owners either to pay rent on land they had owned for generations or to move away.

THE DUST-BOWL

In the mid 1930s, in Colorado, Kansas, South Dakota, New Mexico, Texas and Oklahoma, a combination of high winds, drought, and too many years of over-grazing and over-ploughing, turned former grasslands into one vast dust-bowl. In 1934 dust-laden winds so darkened the skies that in the towns of Oklahoma

CONTRASTING LIVES **The drought of the 1930s that affected parts of America left Europe untouched. The Scottish croft (above) has sturdy children and healthy cattle while the Oklahoma farmer (right) had to shoot his starving cattle.**

streetlights had to be kept on day and night. This was the disaster that led thousands of small farmers to pack up their belongings and head for California with their families, the journey immortalised in John Steinbeck's novel *The Grapes of Wrath*.

' "I like to think how nice it's gonna be, maybe in California," Ma Joad said, "Never cold. An' fruit ever' place, and people just bein' in the nicest places, little white houses in among the orange trees." '

Steinbeck's Joad family were 'Okies' from Oklahoma, but the great westward migration of the mid 1930s flowed from a huge area of the United States. In one county of Texas alone, the population fell abruptly from 40 000 to less than 1000. Once they reached California most of the migrants found poorly paid work as pickers on the fruit farms.

Agricultural depression was a worldwide phenomenon. In France, Italy and Germany, which still had rural economies, it struck at tens of thousands of peasant smallholders, and in Germany even the great feudal estates of the Junkers, east of the Elbe, on which so many livelihoods depended, fell so deeply into debt that they had to receive government subsidies in the Weimar era. Traditional village societies were already disintegrating as young men

and women drifted into the towns seeking paid jobs in industry; faced with unemployment in the early 1930s, many of them were forced to return to their villages, frustrated and discontented. Others began to combine agricultural work with part-time jobs in the town. In France, between 1931 and 1935 peasant incomes fell by a third; in Germany, resentment over falling prices, and wider anxieties about the modernisation and industrialisation of the country, made many peasants turn towards the doctrine of 'Blood and Soil' and some into strong supporters of Nazism. In Britain, too, which still had an agricultural population of over 1 million, prices and land values fell through the floor. The price of wheat dropped to one-sixth of its prewar level, and although the setting up of marketing boards in the early 1930s eased the situation, over 3 million acres of land went out of cultivation. Competition from imported grain from Australia and Canada forced

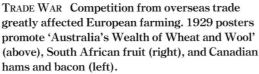

TRADE WAR Competition from overseas trade greatly affected European farming. 1929 posters promote 'Australia's Wealth of Wheat and Wool' (above), South African fruit (right), and Canadian hams and bacon (left).

many farmers to turn to livestock, or fruit-growing and market-gardening to supply the canning industry.

THE MECHANISED FARM

The Depression delayed what would otherwise have been the most striking feature of agriculture in the years between the wars: its mechanisation. On the larger farms of the United States, Canada and Australia, the tractor and the combine harvester had come to dominate the landscape by the 1930s. In Britain, too, although there were only 200 tractors in the entire country in 1930, machines became steadily more familiar features, along with the increasing use of artificial fertilisers. A few farms in East Anglia and Hampshire were almost wholly mechanised.

But everywhere in Europe little had changed since the 19th century. The French farmer might go to market in a petrol-driven car or truck, but otherwise he ran his farm much as his grandfather had done. The horse, or even the ox, could still be seen pulling the plough and the wagon. German farmers who produced surpluses for the market were still known as 'horse farmers'; those who used oxen as draught animals were known as 'cow farmers'; those who had no draught animals at all were known as 'goat farmers'. The harvest also was still conducted much as it had been in the 19th century, and the process of pulling up hedges to make room for machines had barely begun. In remote parts of Britain, despite the Agricultural Wages Act which established minimum terms of employment, even the traditional hiring fair, at which labourers waited to be signed on for a season's work, persisted right up until the end of the 1930s.

OUTDOOR PURSUITS

The British countryside was changing. Thanks to better roads and more use of motorised transport, town and country were meeting as they had never done before. Farmworkers might take a bus to the nearest town at the end of the working day and spend their evening at the cinema instead of in the village pub; it was noticed too that they had largely given up their traditional diet of homemade bread, cheese and beer in favour of the urban worker's tea, white bread and canned food.

More and more townspeople decided to make their homes in the country, or visited it in their cars at weekends, when parties of ramblers – a very popular pastime in this era – were to be seen everywhere. However, due in large part to their relative poverty, farms and farming country in the 1920s and 30s still retained much of its picturesque character from earlier times.

DEPRESSION TIME **The mother and children of a migrant agricultural worker in California in the mid 1930s.**

In the years between the wars, there was some progress towards a more equal distribution of income, in all the countries of the Western world, but very little towards equal distribution of wealth. In the United States and most of the countries of Europe 1 per cent of the population still owned more than 55 per cent of the wealth; in the United States it was nearly 60 per cent. In Britain the richest 5 per cent owned nearly 80 per cent of all wealth, whereas the total value of all the possessions of three-quarters of the population was probably less than £100; compared with today, ordinary people owned very few possessions of any kind.

Membership of the richest 1 per cent was not the same as it had been in 1900, however. Many of the old landed nobility, especially in Britain and Germany, had been severely hit by agricultural depression and rising labour costs. The British novelist Dornford Yates described the fictitious but not untypical case of Sir Anthony Bagot and his estate, called Merry Down:

'One of the old school, Sir Anthony had stood his ground up to the last. The War had cost him dear. His only son was killed in the first months. His only grandson fell in the battles of the Somme. His substance, never fat, had shrunk to a mere shadow of its former self. The stout old heart fought the unequal fight month after month. Stables were emptied, rooms were shut up, thing after thing was sold. It remained for a defaulting solicitor to administer the *coup de grace*. . . . On the twelfth day of August . . . Merry Down was to be sold by auction.'

THE PROBLEMS OF THE RICH

Many of the heirs of the landed class – British, French and German – had indeed perished in the Great War. In Germany the nobility clung to their castles and their estates and struggled to maintain a feudal lifestyle, but unless they had also involved themselves in commerce, they found themselves sinking deep into debt. In Britain landed estates were being sold off; the Duke of Rutland sold half of the Belvoir estate, and the Duke of Sutherland disposed of over a quarter of a million acres in Scotland. Some of the very biggest landowners were still among the very wealthiest men in the land by 1940, but the fortunes of the landed gentry in general had declined.

On the other hand, thousands of new fortunes had been created, mainly in North America but in Europe too, and many of these were in finance and commerce rather than in manufacturing industry. The largest fortune left in Britain between the wars was that of Sir John Ellerman, shipowner and financier (£36.7 million); the second largest that of the brewer Edward Guinness, 1st Earl of Iveagh (£13.5 million); and the third that of James Williamson, 1st Baron Ashton, a linoleum manufacturer (£10.5 million).

Merchants, bankers, shipowners, stockbrokers and insurers accounted for 40 per cent of all British millionaires in the interwar years. The estates of just four millionaires in 1938-9 were worth more than those of 85 000 of the poorest who died then. Even so, the fortunes accumulated in Britain were dwarfed by those built up by some continental industrialists and financiers who had a lighter tax burden, or in the United States by men like John Pierpoint Morgan or Henry Rockefeller. The richest American millionaires, it was calculated, were on average ten or twenty times wealthier than their British counterparts. And marriages between rich American heiresses and the relatively impoverished heirs of ancient British and continental lands and titles were a common feature of the interwar years.

Even the immensely wealthy could no longer live in quite the same luxurious and ostentatious style of their parents or grandparents in the Edwardian period. London 'Society', for example, in the sense of a titled, landed class able to throw open great town houses for large social gatherings in 'the Season', had largely disappeared. The 6th Duke of Portland listed only Londonderry, Apsley, Bridgewater and Holland House as private residences in London in the mid 1930s, compared with more than a dozen houses he had owned in 1914, and he was considered exceptional in having so many.

A BUDGET FOR THE UNEMPLOYED

IN 1939, the British magazine *Picture Post* listed the weekly expenditure of Alfred Smith, an unemployed man of 35 with wife and four children.

His weekly benefit amounted to £2 7s 6d, rather more than most unemployed men because three of his children were sickly. He kept a shilling or so for fares, tobacco and newspapers and handed the rest over to his wife, who spent it as follows:

Rent	14s 6d
Clothes clubs	6s 0d
Insurance	1s 8d
Coal club	2s 0d
Coke	1s 0d
Lighting and fittings	3s 0d
Bread	6s 0d
Other food	16s 0d
Total	£2 10s 2d

The budget left the Smiths with a deficit of about 4s a week. They said that the only way they could live was by getting into debt, and that if they needed to make any extra expenditure, for example on items such as shoes, the only way they were able to meet it was by cutting down on necessities like food or fuel.

YOU RANG, SIR?

P.G. WODEHOUSE'S view of the upper classes and their servants was based on his experience of life in England before the First World War. Bertie Wooster, whom Wodehouse records as never having done a day's paid work, was already becoming an untypical figure in the 1920s and represented a type that had virtually disappeared by the 1930s.

There were still personal man-servants on the Jeeves model, but very few of them would be in the service of a young bachelor such as Wooster; they were more likely by this time to be in the employment of American millionaires. The 'World of Wooster', as Wodehouse admirers recognised, was a world of fantasy.

Americans as a whole relied less on domestic service than in the 19th century, but in Britain and conti-nental Europe, the numbers of serv-ants employed overall had not greatly declined. In wealthy upper-class households, there was still an 'upstairs' and a 'downstairs' world, the latter being the place where the mundane tasks of life were discreetly carried out by paid employees.

DIFFERENT WORLDS Life in an upper-class house is conducted on two levels. Right, P.G. Wodehouse in his sports tourer, 1928.

In Britain, the Prince of Wales consorted with people from a wider range of social backgrounds than even his grandfather, King Edward VII, who had been notable for including people who had made their fortunes in 'trade' among his friends. The Prince was a leading member of the new, rather looser form of Anglo-European 'Society' that frequented restaurants and nightclubs and included filmstars and industrialists, as well as members of the old landed aristocracy. Chips Channon, the Conservative MP, described one evening in 1934:

'Dinner was staggering, champagne flowed and the food was excellent. We began with blinis served with Swedish schnapps, to wash down the caviare. The soup, followed by salmon, then an elaborate chicken. Then a sweet and savoury. The candlelight was reflected in my gold plate and the conversation was incessant.'

CLASS AND CASTE

Now that wealth was not necessarily associated with the ownership of land or ancient title, 'the rich' were no longer a coherent group within society. Oxford-educated clergymen now earned less than some skilled industrial workers; men of lowly origins could become millionaires; and many ex-officers begged in the streets. 'Class' could no longer be identified with relative wealth, and, in Britain in particular, there was an increased interest in what can only be called 'caste', with all its subtle nuances of accent, manners and dress. The old-Etonian socialist writer George Orwell, exploring the lower depths of society in the 1930s, came upon a drunk in a London dosshouse; within moments he had identified him, from his accent and the quality of his shoes, as a 'gentleman' and a fellow Etonian. People of all classes were readily able to assign themselves or others to 'rough' or 'respectable' working class, or lower-middle or middle-middle class by means of similar codes.

HIGH LIFE A game of backgammon at the Rainbow Room, the 'world's highest nightclub', situated at the top of a New York skyscraper.

THE GREAT DEPRESSION

The Wall Street Crash of 1929 produced worldwide misery.

Mass unemployment drove many to consider extreme solutions.

IN 1932 the popular singer Rudy Vallee was asked by President Hoover to sing something that would take people's minds off the worries of the Great Depression that had begun with the Wall Street Crash of 1929; instead, he sang the song that summed up for many the agony of those times: 'Buddy, can you spare a dime?' It was about a man who had helped to build the American Dream and now found himself reduced to begging in the street. There were many such in 1932, the worst year of the Depression. Between 15 and 17 million men were unemployed, and since most of them represented families, that meant that millions more were plunged into poverty. *Fortune* magazine estimated that year that 34 million Americans were without any income whatsoever, and that figure excluded 11 million farming families, most of whom were also reduced to a state of penury.

There was no unemployment pay, and strong opposition to suggestions that there should be. Responsibility for public aid was left to private charities and local authorities, if they could find the money. With some honourable exceptions, the rich showed themselves cruelly indifferent to the problem. All classes were affected: New York department stores were demanding college degrees from those seeking work as elevator operators; on Long Island a registered nurse was found starving on a private estate where she had slept for two weeks wrapped in newspapers and rags. Hundreds slept rough in the city parks; thousands, unable to find even a soup kitchen, rooted for food in garbage pails; in country districts they ate weeds. Men without work developed new skills for keeping alive. A man with a nickel could buy

THE GREAT CRASH Panic outside the Wall Street Stock Exchange as the stock market collapses in October 1929.

ON THE BREADLINE Priests of the New Hope mission in New York distribute bread during the Depression. The smiling faces are not typical.

a cup of coffee, then ask for another cup of hot water free; by mixing the water with the tomato ketchup on the counter he could make a kind of soup. Newspapers stuffed under the shirt kept out the worst of the cold; and shoes could be lined with cardboard. People sold their most precious possessions to buy food for their children. Many died from exposure, and a large proportion of the population was suffering severe malnutrition. Others committed suicide rather than face the shame of going on public relief.

Two million Americans, mostly men, were living like nomads in 1932, crossing and recrossing the country, often clinging to the rods under railroad cars, in a desperate search for work. Some states posted armed guards on the highways to turn them away; local authorities charged impoverished strangers with vagrancy and threw them out of town

or into jail; for many this was welcome, since it offered shelter and basic food. An employment agency in Manhattan had 5000 applications for 300 jobs. An Arkansas man walked 900 miles (1448 km) looking for work. In Washington men were reported to be starting forest fires so that they would be hired to put them out. In the early 1930s emigration from the United States exceeded immigration; in New York there were 350 applications a day from people wanting to emigrate to the Soviet Union.

Many thousands of dispossessed farmers, facing financial ruin after three years of drought,

SOUP KITCHEN
Out-of-work
American men eat
bread and soup at
a kitchen during
the Depression.

which compounded the effects of the Depression, joined the breadlines or packed their households into Model T Fords and headed West to find work as fruitpickers in California.

The Depression, bad enough elsewhere in the world, was a calamity for the United States. Apart from the absence of federal welfare provision, which led so many into destitution, the psychological effects were traumatic, many of the jobless suffered feelings of guilt about their inability to provide for themselves or their families. At the fringes of society a minority became convinced that only Marxism or fascism could solve the problems that seemed to have brought the country to the brink of disaster. The majority instead voted in 1932 for President Roosevelt and his New Deal policies of welfare and public works. These did not produce immediate results as progress was slow, and in 1937-8 there was another trough of depression, when 5 million people who had obtained jobs in the New Deal era again found themselves unemployed. Those who had suffered so badly clung to the belief that, in time, things would get better. Thanks in part to rearmament for the Second World War, they did.

At the same time, some of the sharper edges of class distinction were being blurred: the new cinemas had different prices in different parts of the house, but they offered much the same level of comfort to all who used them, whether rich or poor; and the chainstores catered to a much wider social spectrum than the working-class corner shop and the exclusive department store.

BRIGHT YOUNG THINGS

In Germany, the hyperinflation of the 1920s virtually wiped out the 'rentier' class – those who lived on the income from capital invested in shares or government stock – but elsewhere there was still a leisured class who did not need to, and did not, work. It was the younger and more frivolous members of this class who became the 'Bright Young Things' of the 1920s, who danced till dawn or were arrested in police raids on nightclubs. This group attracted the hostility of the Marxist Left, but for most people in the 1920s its existence was unquestioningly accepted as a fact of life; its doings were read about in novels (P.G. Wodehouse's Bertie Wooster was a representative example) or in the gossip columns of newspapers, or seen in the cinema, without resentment and with amusement. The society photographer Cecil Beaton described a typical 1920s party in *Vogue* magazine:

'... people literally overflowing into the street ... all the people one had ever known or even seen – up and down the big staircase, in the ballroom, along the corridors – "Hutch" singing in the ballroom while we all sat on the floor – Edythe Baker playing to some of us in another room downstairs – Oliver Messel in the same room giving a ludicrously lifelike imitation of a lift-attendant describing the departments on each floor – Lady Ashley shining in a glittering short coat of silver sequins over her white dress – glimpses of the Ruthven twins – of Noel Coward looking happy and being amusing – Gladys Cooper in a Chanel rhinestone necklace that reached to the knees of her black velvet frock ...'

HAPPY FAMILY The comparatively untroubled lifestyle of an upper-middle class English family of the 1920s is caught in this magazine illustration which portrays wireless as a medium of musical education.

This, for a handful of years in the 1920s, was the everyday life of a section of the privileged leisured class, whether in New York, London or Paris. In the 1930s, with the spectacle of so much misery on the streets, there was a growing feeling that the open display of wealthy frivolity was an affront to the jobless and the poor, and that men, at least, should take up some kind of paid employment if they could find it.

But Hollywood still found it worth while to portray characters on the screen – played perhaps by Fred Astaire and Ginger Rogers – who floated through life without a care in the world. They provided the glamour and carefree happiness that people seemed to need in order to escape, if only for a few hours, from the anxious and shabby world outside the cinema.

THE UPPER-MIDDLE CLASSES

During the interwar years, the well-to-do upper-middle class – for example, those employed in the higher reaches of business, the civil service and the professions – could still lead comfortable lives.

The writer David Thomson recalled breakfast in the 1920s at the home of his great-uncle Robert, a Scottish judge. First the family, guests and servants met in the dining room for morning prayers:

'And then, the crowd of ladies' maids, housemaids, tablemaids, kitchen and scullery maids were always marched out by Mrs Waddell before breakfast began. The butlers, valets and under-butlers, the gardener, under-gardener and lesser outdoor men marched after them to breakfast in the servants' hall. . . .

'Uncle Robert ate a prodigious breakfast. . . . After his porridge he had two boiled eggs, then Arbroath smokies, Finnan haddock or a pair of Nairn speldings,

HIGH SOCIETY Baron van der Elst in his open tourer, with his fiancée Miss Roebling and her hounds. They give every sign of fitting happily into Washington's leisured class of the 1920s.

then steak, kidneys with bacon, or two mutton chops. He ate slowly. It took him at least an hour.'

It was beginning to be unusual to have so many servants in just one household. There were under 2 million servants in the USA by 1932, but there were still rather more proportionately in Britain and Europe. The 'servant problem' – the difficulty of finding and keeping good ones – was a frequent topic of conversation in those years. But most upper-middle-class households still employed at least three or four: inside the house a cook and a housemaid, neatly dressed in a black dress and a white cap and apron; outside, a gardener and perhaps a chauffeur. (The chauffeur's uniform of breeches and high boots or leather gaiters reflected the fact that his predecessor of only a few years before had been a coachman or a groom.)

Members of the upper-middle classes could still maintain, and build, substantial houses. They were the owners of tennis courts and the patrons of golf clubs. They ordered their groceries by telephone, dressed for dinner, even when dining privately at home, and were among the relatively small number of people who took their holidays abroad. Even if they employed fewer servants of their own, they enjoyed an abundance of deferential service from tradespeople, shop assistants, delivery boys and workers on the railways and in the postal service. David Thomson's father, an army officer, could not afford to travel first class on the railway with his family when they went on holiday, but they could enjoy the convenience of having their luggage collected:

'The start of our excitement was the arrival of the little bus which Father ordered from the railway company. It was made of brown varnished wood with

RUSH HOUR During a strike in Germany in 1922 an overcrowded train prepares to leave for Berlin. Usually, trains provided comfortable, reliable transport.

big windows and a luggage rack on the roof. The driver and one porter who rode with him went upstairs when they arrived and carried down our trunks, then went back for the valises and suitcases, bicycles, pram, pushcarts, which were in the hall. Our parents carried the smaller things like golf clubs, hat boxes and fishing rods, and we looked after the animals – two dogs on leads, thirteen guinea pigs and two tortoises in baskets. Then the bus carried us all to the bustle of porters and passengers at Euston.'

THE MIDDLE-MIDDLE CLASSES

Especially in the prosperous parts of Britain and North America, and in countries such as Australia, New Zealand and South Africa, the class that most benefited from increasing affluence in the interwar years was what might be called the middle-middle class – the growing numbers of salaried people such as civil servants, teachers, and managerial and clerical workers. However, most European countries lagged behind in this middle-middle-class growth, either because of economic distress, as in Germany, or because they were as yet much less industrialised.

With smaller families and an increasing income in real terms, these newly prosperous middle-middle classes were in the best possible position to enjoy the benefits of the new 'consumer' society: they were the purchasers of the new suburban houses, the new motor cars, the new consumer durables and of leisure and entertainment opportunities. Demanding good education for their children, and able to pay for it, they actually increased the number of private, fee-paying schools in Britain, while in North America they could finance the provision of teaching aids, gymnasiums and sports facilities in local schools. In Britain they also employed domestic servants, and benefited from the new labour-saving devices.

Whereas the average number of servants per household had fallen, the total number of households employing servants probably increased, particularly in Britain, where in 1931 at least one family in five had one or more living-in domestics; many others had a visiting 'daily' to help with the cooking and cleaning. As a result, the total number of servants employed in that year was marginally higher than in the years immediately before the First World War.

EMPLOYMENT AND UNEMPLOYMENT

Those men and women who were able to find and keep good employment in the interwar years enjoyed a steady increase in their standard of living. Although the Depression blighted large parts of the country, especially in the traditional industrial areas, the overall picture in Britain and North America was one of economic growth; real wages rose, working hours were shorter, and the cost of living actually fell by more than a third between 1920 and 1939.

Combined with smaller average families, the increase in earnings meant that a majority of people had surplus spending power, and the time to spend it on leisure activities and on improving their homes. In 1914, for example, the average working-class family had devoted more than 75 per cent of its income to food and rent; by the end of the 1930s the proportion had fallen to around 45 per cent. The surplus income could be spent on fuel and light, clothing, household goods, a wider range of foodstuffs, and entertainment; it financed the creation of the first mass consumer society, which in itself created new jobs. Despite the many instances of low pay, the effects of improved living standards could be seen everywhere. Even in

JARROW MARCH Unemployed men from Jarrow march to London in 1926 to advertise their plight.

Glasgow, hit badly by the Depression in the 1930s, the writer Thomas Jones could note: 'Food is more varied. Fresh fruit is available all the year round. The milk supply is cleaner, and the byres have been driven beyond the city bounds. Drunkenness has diminished, and the scandalous scenes witnessed on Saturday nights in Argyll Street seem so far away and long ago.

'. . . Barefooted women and children were common in the eighties. No one sees them today. The shawl has gone and the hat has taken its place . . . working girls, who then tidied themselves only for special occasions, are now always neatly dressed and are careful of their hair and teeth and fingernails – a great change.'

And the historian Sidney Pollard writes of this period in general: 'Statistics fail to take full account of the difference made by electricity instead of candles, and gas cookers instead of coal or coke ranges, as standard equipment in working-class homes; of improved housing, including indoor water and sanitation; or of radio, the cinema and newspapers within almost everybody's reach.'

These improvements, particularly striking to anyone who had known the condition of the working class before the First World War, could be seen everywhere in the industrialised countries of the world.

THE POOR AND UNEMPLOYED

While the majority of people enjoyed improved living standards in the 1930s a significant minority lived in poverty, mainly as a result of unemployment. In Britain in the winter of 1932-3, 3 million people, a quarter of the workforce, were unemployed; in the United States the figure was over 15 million, again

"Mates! help me get a job."

VOTE – FOR THE NATIONAL GOVERNMENT

CRISIS GOVERNMENT In 1931 a coalition National Government, led by Ramsay MacDonald, was elected to solve the economic crisis.

perhaps a quarter of the workforce; in Germany there were 5.6 million registered unemployed, almost a third of the workforce, and probably another million unregistered; and in Australia unemployment rose to over 25 per cent. By the summer of 1933, when things began to improve slightly, many people could look back on four years without work.

Even these figures are misleading. They do not include the millions of small farmers facing ruin, or the small tradesmen whose businesses were devastated by the cuts in working-class spending, or the public employees, such as teachers, civil servants, policemen, who were forced to take severe salary cuts.

Most of the industrialised countries of Europe paid some form of state unemployment benefit, but generally only to male industrial workers, and not to women, farmworkers, domestic servants or to those who had been self-employed. Where benefits were paid, they were barely enough to keep families above starvation level. They were also strictly means-tested; inspectors regularly visited the homes of claimants to check whether they had any other form of income, or any goods that might be sold.

THE MEANS TEST

The Means Test was everywhere loathed for its intrusiveness and the way it deprived unemployed men of the last shreds of dignity. On one of the hunger marches in 1930s Britain the marchers brought with them a petition for the abolition of means-testing, said to carry 1 million signatures, which they intended to present to Parliament. The bulky document was deposited for safety in a railway left luggage office, where it mysteriously disappeared, although the ticket had not been lost; it was believed that the disappearance had been contrived by the authorities, to avoid parliamentary embarrassment. Statistics do not fully convey the psychological effects of long-term unemployment: the burden of shame and uselessness, the terrible state of apathy into which many fell, or the condition of shabby neglect that ran through entire communities. In Germany, where the effects of unemployment were particularly severe, many young men joined the street gangs of the extreme Left and Right, in many cases simply as a way of filling up time during the day and working off their feelings of impotent rage. By 1932 the German Communist Party was almost entirely a party of the unemployed.

THE REALITY OF POVERTY

Poverty was defined in surveys of the time as the level at which almost any incidental expense meant less to eat: at which, for example, a choice had to be made between buying fuel for heating and cooking and buying food. Perhaps 10 per cent of the population of Britain lived at this level in the inter-war years; in Germany rather more. In the United States in 1932 *Fortune* magazine estimated that 34 million men, women and children – almost 28 per cent of the population – had no income whatsoever. In that year the New York City Health Department reported that over 20 per cent of pupils in the public schools were suffering from malnutrition. The American Friends Service Committee reported that in the mining areas of states such as Virginia, Kentucky and Pennsylvania the level of malnourished children might be as high as 90 per cent, the children showing telltale signs of 'lethargy and sleepiness' and 'mental retardation'. When a teacher suggested that it would be best for one small girl to go home and get something to eat, the child replied: 'I can't. This is my sister's day to eat.' Teachers and policemen were

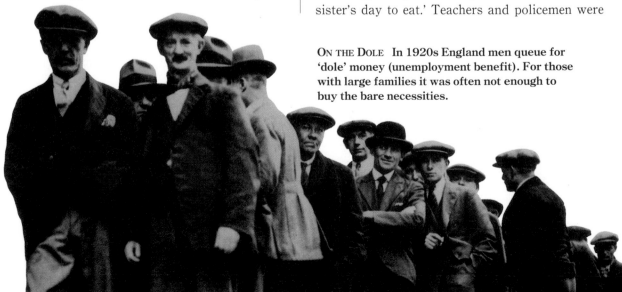

ON THE DOLE In 1920s England men queue for 'dole' money (unemployment benefit). For those with large families it was often not enough to buy the bare necessities.

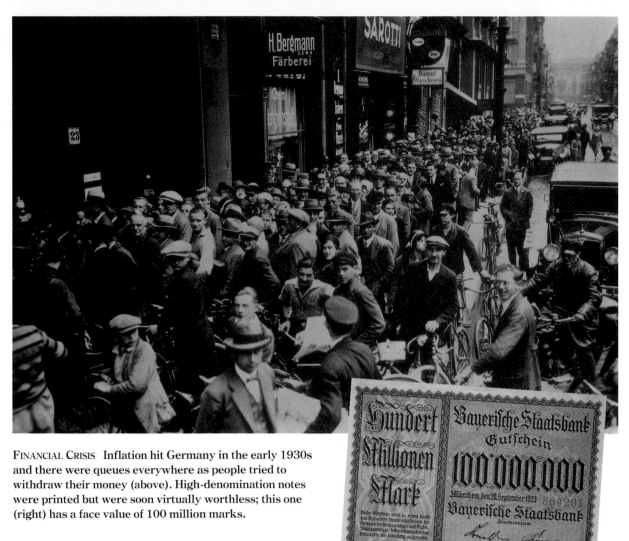

FINANCIAL CRISIS Inflation hit Germany in the early 1930s and there were queues everywhere as people tried to withdraw their money (above). High-denomination notes were printed but were soon virtually worthless; this one (right) has a face value of 100 million marks.

among those who saw this kind of poverty at first hand. Although poorly paid themselves, they often did more than the rich to try to alleviate conditions. Policemen, for example, put whatever they could spare into funds for providing boots and shoes for poor children.

The poor generally consisted of the elderly, the chronically ill, widows with young children, and those who suffered from a combination of unemployment or low pay and large families. The elderly, for instance, received state pensions in most Western European countries, but at a level (£1 per week for a married couple in Britain) which meant that, if they had no other income and could not find rent-free housing, they fell below the poverty line. Similarly, widows who had any significant earnings were obliged to forfeit their widow's pension; most therefore had to choose between eking out a living on a pension or accepting menial low-paid work. The situation was such that chronic illness for the wage-earner in a working-class family could mean destitution. The mass unemployment of the 1930s came on top of a situation in which millions of families were already living at or below the poverty line. This kind of poverty, hidden away in the slum areas of major cities or country districts, was often invisible. But some of it became visible at the outbreak of war in 1939 when a million children and their mothers were evacuated, many from the slums, to homes in safe areas. Middle-class people for the first time saw children with head lice, impetigo and scabies, often unwashed. Many were '. . . not only very badly equipped, but they brought no change of clothes and the garments they wore often had to be burnt as they were verminous. In other cases, the householders had to keep the children in bed while they washed their clothes. Some children arrived sewn into a piece of calico with a coat on top and no other clothes at all.' Some mothers told their children to defecate on newspaper and then burn it on the fire, a habit attributed to their experience of the filthy, shared outdoor lavatories in the slum districts.

TRANSPORT AND TRAVEL

Whether by train, ship, aeroplane or in a luxury motor car,

travel had never been so pleasant as it was in the 1920s and 30s –

for those who could afford it.

MORE people than ever before travelled in the interwar years and, because of technical innovations, could do so in relative comfort and safety. In all the countries of Europe and North America in the 1920s the railway network reached its fullest extent, still scarcely challenged by the motor car for long-distance overland travel; and almost every town had its railway station.

Motorways were being built, first in Italy and then in Germany, but elsewhere roads still passed mainly through the centres of villages and towns and were not yet well suited to long-distance, high-speed travel; even in the United States, it was difficult to average more than 250 miles (402 km) in a full day's drive, until the mid 1930s. Although more and more suburban lines were electrified, most main-line trains were still hauled by steam locomotives. Far from being regarded as an outmoded means of transport, they were constantly being improved, and the locomotives of the 1930s could easily maintain average speeds of over 80 mph (129 km/h) – in July 1938 the British *Mallard*, designed by Sir

STICKER No item of luggage was complete unless it was covered with labels like this.

Nigel Gresley and hauling a seven-coach train, reached a speed of 125 mph (201 km/h), the highest ever achieved by a steam locomotive. In the 1930s, under American influence, engines such as the A4 type were covered in streamlined fairings which, while hardly affecting performance, gave them an exciting, 'futuristic' appearance.

Even the moderately well-off could travel in considerable luxury in the 1920s and 30s. North American trains offered Pullman cars, sleeping cars, club cars and observation platforms; and the restaurant cars of the trans-European expresses provided excellent food in elegant surroundings. The Orient Express was the supreme example of luxury travel by rail, but even lesser trains made use of inlaid wood, etched glass, table lamps, dazzling white napery and polished tableware in the company's livery.

STREAMLINER Henry Dreyfuss designed the streamlining for this New York Central locomotive. It and others like it hauled the 'Twentieth Century Limited', the stylish New York–Chicago express.

SPEED AND COMFORT The 'Coronation' London to Scotland express was hauled by locomotives like the record-breaking *Mallard*. The coaches were luxuriously appointed (top right) and, unusually for Great Britain, included an observation lounge (left).

Scheduled air services, which had begun soon after the First World War, grew steadily between the wars. In Europe, air travel was relatively expensive and was used mainly by businessmen and rich people in a hurry; only in North America was an attempt made to offer a service on domestic flights that, although not luxurious, compared in price with rail fares. The planes of the time were remarkably safe – the huge biplanes of the state-owned British line, Imperial Airways, flew a total of some 10 million miles to Europe and the Middle East without losing a single passenger – but they were still relatively slow and uncomfortable, and cabins were unpressurised and unheated. Only the flying boats, which supplied long-distance services, offered adequate space and headroom. The Short Brothers' Empire Flying-Boats of Imperial Airways had a spacious promenade deck and smoking cabin, and the Pan American Boeing 314, which inaugurated the first transatlantic service in 1939, offered her 19 passengers separate cabin accommodation, a dining saloon, a ladies' dressing room, a recreation lounge and a bridal suite. Flying-boat travel to the Far East and Australia, with its overnight stops in exotic locations, was an enjoyable and leisurely experience.

Airports were relatively small and simple affairs, consisting of little more than a control tower, hangars, fuel tanks, and a waiting room for passengers, who walked out to the planes while airline staff carried their luggage. Britain's leading airport, Croydon, which opened in 1928, cost £260 000 to build, and that included the construction of a 50-bedroom hotel.

Flying was regarded as a sporting activity. Until 1931 enthusiasts avidly followed the contests run for the Schneider Trophy. The final Schneider contest was won by R.J. Mitchell's Supermarine seaplane (an ancestor of the wartime Spitfire) which set a speed record of 406.94 mph (654.89 km/h). Other records were established later in the 1930s: an altitude record of 49 967 ft (15 230 m) in 1936 and a distance

ON A DIFFERENT TRACK

For publicity purposes in the 1930s, some British locomotives and coaches were sent to America to show their paces. They performed well and their styling was much admired but, although the track gauge is the same, Americans were unable to respond as their locomotives and coaches were too wide and high for European railways.

CORONATION
THE FIRST STREAMLINE TRAIN
KINGS CROSS FOR SCOTLAND

LONDON & NORTH EASTERN RAILWAY

EXPRESS TRAIN
Most locomotives in the inter-war years were not streamlined, but they set speed records just the same.

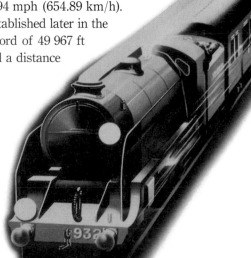

THE HINDENBURG DISASTER

ON MAY 6, 1937 an American radio-news reporter was watching as the German airship *Hindenburg* came in to land at Lakehurst, New Jersey. As he watched the disaster, choking with emotion, his words were recorded:

❝ Here in Lakehurst it's starting to rain again, the rain had slacked up a bit. The back motors of the *Hindenburg* are just holding it, just enough to keep it from – It's bursting into flames! Get that shot! Get that shot! It's cra-crashing, crashing, terrible, oh my, get out of the way please, it's burning, bursting into flames, and is falling on the mooring paths and all the people agree this is one of the terrible, worst tragedies of the world! Oh, flames four or five hundred feet into the sky, it's a terrific crash, ladies and gentlemen, the smoke and the flames now and the crashing to the ground, not quite to the mooring, oh the humanity, and I told you, I can't even talk, mass of smoking wreckage, I can, I can hardly breathe, ohh, ohhh, ohhh. ❞

DEATH OF AN AIRSHIP The giant German airship *Hindenburg* crashes while landing at Lakehurst, New Jersey.

record of 7162 miles (11 526 km) in 1938. All over the Western world, members of private flying clubs were discovering the joys of flying for the sheer fun of it. But, knowingly or unknowingly, the flying skills they were acquiring were also preparing them to be the fighter pilots of the Second World War.

In the 1920s the airship seemed to promise a new era of safe, pleasant and comfortable travel. But, so far as Britain was concerned, that future came to an abrupt halt on October 5, 1930, when the R101 – of which it had been said that 'the comfort of the passenger quarters is little short of a miracle' –

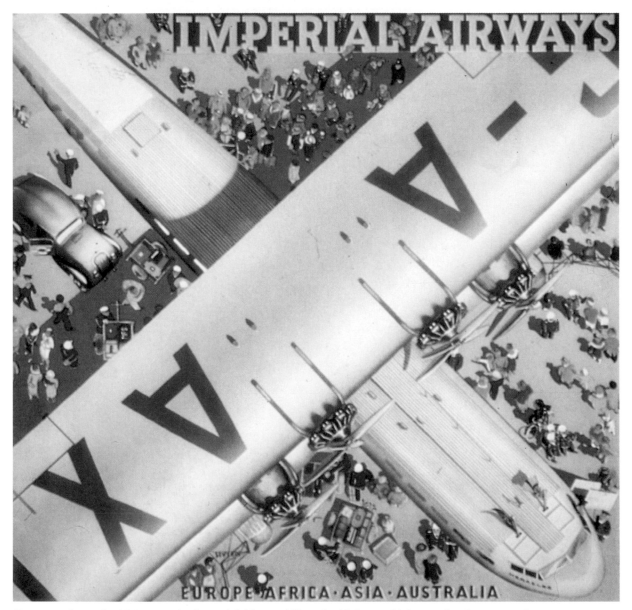

EUROPE · AFRICA · ASIA · AUSTRALIA

SLOW BUT SURE A 1934 poster for Imperial Airways' Heracles biplane, which was slow but very safe.

crashed near Beauvais on a trial flight from Cardington to India. The 46 people who lost their lives in the disaster included the British Air Minister, Lord Thomson, and most of the Air Ministry's airship experts.

Then on May 6, 1937, the *Hindenburg*, a giant German airship which the previous year had crossed the Atlantic in 46 hours, burst into flames as it was coming in to land at Lakehurst, New Jersey, with 97 people on board. This second disaster brought the brief airship era to an end.

AIR RACE The Schneider Trophy contest, 1929. In such competitions the fighter planes of the Second World War were born.

IN-FLIGHT SERVICE

The first air hostess was Miss Ellen Church, who started work for United Airlines in May 1931. She had been hired at her own suggestion. As well as serving a standard meal of fruit cocktail, fried chicken and tea or coffee, duties included helping to push the aircraft in and out of hangars. Air France recruited air hostesses in 1931, Swissair in 1934, KLM in 1935 and Lufthansa in 1938. Britain employed only male cabin staff until 1943.

THE HEIGHT OF COMFORT   The sleeping compartment of a Fokker F-32. Few planes had this kind of comfort. In a 1920s poster (right) a couple fly the Lufthansa symbol.

By 1938 it was possible to fly from Britain to Australia without having to change aircraft, and Pan American World Airways had regular trans-Pacific mail and passenger flights. But the most favoured means of leisured inter-continental travel was the ocean-going liner. Liners of the period,

SAFE FLIGHT! Waving goodbye at Tempelhof airport (above) as a Lufthansa plane prepares for takeoff in 1928. A Caproni flying boat (right), designed to carry 100 passengers, on a test flight over Lake Maggiore in 1921.

especially those on the North Atlantic run, reached superb heights of elegance and luxury, comparable with anything to be found in the best international hotels. Passengers on the German *Europa* and *Bremen*, the French *Ile de France* and *Normandie*, the British *Queen Mary* or the Italian *Rex* and *Conti di Savoia* could pass the voyage pleasantly in ballrooms, gymnasiums, swimming pools, libraries and excellent restaurants, conceived and built by some of the best artists, designers and craftsmen of the day using only the best materials.

THE AUTOMOBILE REVOLUTION

The main development in transport between the wars was the huge growth in private automobile ownership. In this, North America took the lead and maintained it. In 1921 one person in 14 in the USA owned a car, as against one in 168 in Britain, and even fewer elsewhere in Europe. In 1930 there were just under a million licensed cars in Britain, roughly one for every 15 households; by 1939 the number in Britain had almost doubled and car-ownership in the USA was almost universal.

The 1920s and 1930s were the era of the luxury grand touring car – the Bentleys, Lagondas, Delages, Bugattis, Mercedes and Hispano-Suizas. Of the last of these, perhaps

A SHRINKING WORLD A 1931 poster for Imperial Airways gives destinations and times of departure from Croydon airport. But air travel was still largely only for the rich.

the most elegant of all, Michael Arlen wrote in his 1924 best-selling novel *The Green Hat*:

'Like a huge yellow insect that had dropped to earth from a butterfly civilisation, this car, gallant and suave, rested in the lowly silence of the Shepherd Market night. Open as a yacht, it wore a great shining bonnet, and flying over the crest of this great bonnet, as though in proud flight over the heads of scores of phantom horses, was that silver stork by which the gentle may be pleased to know that they have just escaped death beneath the wheels of a Hispano-Suiza car.'

Many of the deluxe cars of the 1920s were exclusively designed by coachbuilders and handmade by craftsmen. Women celebrities had their cars painted and upholstered to match the colours of their favourite clothes, or, in the case of the black American singer and dancer Josephine Baker, her skin. Their prices put them far beyond the means of all but the very rich. But this was also the era of the cheap popular car, *(continued on page 108)*

LIFE ABOARD A CUNARD LINER

HOLDER of the blue riband for the fastest crossing of the Atlantic in 1936, the luxury ship the *Queen Mary* was launched by Queen Mary herself in December 1934. Her fastest-ever crossing of the Atlantic was at a speed of 31.69 knots. Like the *Normandie*, her near-contemporary and rival, the *Queen Mary* offered the ultimate in luxury and contemporary design, despite the fact that both ships were built in the midst of the Depression. The *Mary* was said to resemble the grand Dorchester Hotel in London. Certainly her facilities were similar to those of the hotel, with a library, a cinema, play rooms for children, a ballroom, luxurious restaurants and bars, a swimming pool and gymnasium, and for first-class passengers, the personal services of a cabin steward 24 hours a day.

THE ONLY WAY TO CROSS

Royalty, millionaires and celebrities were among the passengers on the great ocean liners, their every whim catered for.

THE great transatlantic liners of the 1920s and 30s were very big and very fast. Writing about the *Normandie* and the *Queen Mary*, the two ships that dominated the 1930s, the American writer Frank Braynard commented that a taxi darting out of the old Pennsylvania station in New York at 32 mph (51.5 km/h) would cause no surprise, but that if you imagined the station itself following at the same speed you would get some idea of the vastness and power of the two great liners.

The *Normandie*, on her maiden voyage in May 1935, took the blue riband after crossing the Atlantic in four days, three hours and 14 minutes. From then until the outbreak of war, although their captains did not admit to racing,

SEA-GOING STYLE Cunard's *Aquitania*, built in 1914, was generally considered the most fashionable transatlantic liner of the 1920s.

she and the *Queen Mary* competed for the record, achieving average speeds of over 31 knots. They were also elegant and luxurious, offering

UNITED AMERICAN LINES
(HARRIMAN LINE)
joint service with
HAMBURG AMERICAN LINE

NO EXPENSE SPARED A 1924 American advertisement (above) and the main lounge of a 1930s liner (left).

first-class passengers a means of travel between the United States and Europe which had all the comfort and style of a great international hotel. The *Normandie*'s dining hall was the biggest ever seen in any ship, three decks high and 100 yards (91.5 m) long (slightly longer than the Hall of Mirrors at Versailles, as the French line's publicity put it), and offering, naturally, superb cuisine. The *Ile de France*'s bar was the biggest on the Atlantic – 27 ft (8 m) long. *Queen Mary* was called by Cunard 'the Ship of Beautiful Woods', from the fact that her passenger compartments were lined with veneers of precious timbers: angelim, ash, beech, avodire, cedar, cherry, burr, tiger oak, pear, satinwood, sycamore and synara. The French line had spent one-tenth of the *Normandie*'s construction cost on interior decoration. An orchestra played in the grill-room at all meals, a symphony orchestra entertained in the main lounge. There were, of course, swimming pools, gymnasiums, ballrooms, libraries, bars and smoking-rooms, even a theatre. On the *Ile de France* there were 390 exquisite first-class staterooms, each individually designed.

The passenger lists included the very rich, and every effort was made to see that their every wish was satisfied. On one particular voyage on the *Ile de France*, a woman passenger at the captain's table mentioned that she loved to hear music in her bath; next morning the captain arranged for her to be serenaded by the ship's orchestra, assembled outside her stateroom. Another passenger, Señora Zelmira Paz de Gainza, regularly made the crossing accompanied by ten maids, a chamberlain, and four cars. The

Prince of Wales travelled with 135 pieces of luggage – and that was not unusual. Captain Harry Grattide described his ship, the *Berengaria*, as: 'principally a gleaming and bejewelled ferry boat for the rich and titled'. Celebrities also made the crossing, and the shipping lines made sure that their presence on board was announced. In one week in 1923 the White Star line carried Dame Nellie Melba, Dame Clara Butt, the wife of Rudolf Valentino, Lloyd George, Pavlova, and the Prince of Wales, travelling incognito as the Duke of Renfrew. When the canine film star Rin-Tin-Tin crossed the Atlantic on the *Berengaria*, his keeper had a first-class ticket, but lived night and day with the dog on the third-class deck.

Also on board most of the great liners were the professional gamblers. Bertram Hayes, captain of the White Star liner *Olympic* noted that most of them had the trademarks of their profession written all over their faces, but there was one who always dressed as a cleric and spent the first days playing with the children on deck; then, having acquainted himself with their fathers, he would make a good haul. Another was a quiet, scholarly looking man, who was a genius with dice. Most became well-known to the stewards, who would greet them as they came on board with the words 'What name this time, sir?'

After the crash of 1929 there were fewer millionaires to make the Atlantic crossing in style. During the Second World War many liners were converted for use as troop-carriers, although the *Normandie* perished in a fire in New York Harbor. After the war they resumed their role, but things, most experienced passengers agreed, were never quite the same.

FRENCH GLORY The *Normandie*, at Le Havre in 1935, prepares for her maiden voyage across the Atlantic.

SPORTING TYPES A lady takes a drive
in a Bentley (above) in 1931.
An early advertisement for an Audi
open tourer (right).

pioneered by Henry Ford's 'Tin Lizzie'.
Mass production offered fewer
opportunities for variation in design,
but the cars were cheap, and got even
cheaper: in 1924 the British Austin
Seven cost £165 but in 1932 it cost just
under £120; in the early 1930s the
Morris Minor and the Ford Eight were on sale in
Britain for £100; and in the United States a Chevrolet
could be bought for $445. By 1929 there were more
than 23 million cars in the United States. Even as
early as 1923 there were two cars for every three
families in 'Middletown', the typical American city
studied by Helen and Robert Lynd, although some of
the working-class families that had cars did not
possess bathtubs. Hitler introduced the Volkswagen,
'the People's Car', in 1938, but only demonstration

models were produced during the Third Reich.

Between these extremes many of the mid price cars
of the 1930s offered the comfort and luxury of leather
upholstery and walnut dashboards with a steady
increase in engineering refinement and efficiency; and
young men without very much money could buy
small inexpensive sports cars, like the much-loved
British MG, often based on components from more
sedate production-line vehicles.

During the course of the inter-war years the major
automobile manufacturers, such as Ford and General
Motors in the USA, Austin and Morris in Britain, and
Renault, Citroen and Peugeot in France steadily
absorbed or drove out of business the large numbers
of small manufacturers which had flourished in the
early years; General Motors even took over the
German company Opel. In the USA in 1919 a car
owner was as likely to have a Lexington, a Maxwell, a

THE PEOPLE'S CAR Adolf Hitler
inspects the new Volkswagen in
1938. The designer, Dr Porsche,
is in attendance.

Briscoe or a Templar as a Dodge, Buick, Chevrolet or Cadillac; in the 1920s it was still possible to buy a Graham, a Pierce Arrow, a Terraplane, a Stutz, an Auburn, an Edward Peerless, a Cord, a Duesenberg, a Franklin or a Locomobile; and in Britain in the 1930s one could choose between, among others, the AC, the Lanchester, the Armstrong Siddeley, the Humber, the Riley and the Alvis. But in the long term, none of these could compete with the majors on price or could offer the same ready availability of spare parts; many had disappeared by 1929, and few survived the 1930s.

From the early 1930s industrialised countries began to adjust to the fact that the motor car was here to stay, and in ever-increasing numbers. Roads were better signposted; major routes were widened and by-passes built; and the first motel was opened in California in 1925. Traffic signals and pedestrian crossings were introduced in towns; speed limits were set; driving tests were introduced; traffic jams and parking problems became a familiar experience, along with traffic accidents, which resulted in 120 000 deaths in Britain alone between the wars.

In Europe the quality of public transport – in the form of suburban and underground railways, buses, trams and trolleys – improved, but in the United States there was an ominous development in the 1920s. General Motors, Standard Oil and Firestone Tires combined to purchase urban electric trolley systems and then dismantled them in order to ensure the future dominance of motor transport. As the American historian Frederick Allen wrote in 1931:

'The inter-urban trolley perished or survived only as a pathetic anachronism. Railroad after railroad gave up its branch lines, or saw its revenues slowly dwindling under the competition of mammoth inter-urban buses and trucks snorting along six-lane concrete highways. The whole country was covered with a network of passenger bus-lines. In thousands of towns, at the beginning of the decade a single traffic officer at the junction of Main Street and Central Street had been sufficient for the control of traffic. By the end of the decade, what a difference! – red and green lights, blinkers, one-way streets, boulevard stops, stringent and yet more stringent parking ordinances – and still a shining flow of traffic that backed up for blocks along Main Street every Saturday and Sunday afternoon. Slowly but surely the age of steam was yielding to the gasoline age.'

By the late 1930s, the shape of the growing cities of the United States was beginning to reflect the fact of almost universal car ownership.

LUXURY LIMOUSINE Until the late 1930s luxury American cars, like this Lincoln, differed little from European cars.

LEISURE AND ENTERTAINMENT

Radio and the cinema dominated the first age of mass leisure and

mass entertainment, but for a time it seemed that everyone was dancing to the

sound of the new American music.

THE 1920s AND 30s were the first age of mass leisure and mass entertainment. Thanks to shorter working hours and increased spending power, ordinary people had more time and money than ever before to spend on fun, and mass communications meant that these pleasures were shared more widely. Nationally, and internationally, people were seeing the same films, playing the same games, dancing to the same music, humming the same hit songs, and admiring the same film and sports heroes.

During the period more and more people were given paid holidays and more of them spent their holidays away from

home. The popular leisure resorts expanded and improved their facilities; fairgrounds, pavilions, bandstands, swimming pools, cinemas, dance halls, tennis courts, and bowling and putting greens became regular features, along with cinemas and bigger and better hotels. New York's Coney Island, for example, became a major amusement centre after the subway reached there in 1920. It added rides, restaurants and souvenir shops to its famous 3 1/2 mile (5.6 km) boardwalk. In Britain, by the late 1930s, more than 20 million visitors a year were going to seaside resorts. Blackpool,

HOLIDAY TIME **Youngsters with bucket and shrimp net, from a railway holiday guide of the 1930s.**

THE WORLD'S FAVOURITE MONSTER

BRITISH popular newspapers of the 1930s loved a sensational story, and few stories were more sensational than that of the Loch Ness Monster.

Legends of a monster in Loch Ness had existed since St Columba's day, and the monks of Fort Augustus on the shore of the loch claimed that most of them had seen it at one time or another. But in the summer of 1933 there were several sightings: an Automobile Association patrolman said he had seen a serpent-like shape in the water. A big-game hunter claimed he had found animal spoor, which the Natural History Museum in London said resembled that of a hippopotamus.

Thousands of tourists were drawn to the loch,

NESSIE SURFACES **and has her picture taken in 1934. The photo was found to be a fake.**

and theories and rumours abounded. Some suggested the creature was a whale which had slipped into the loch when young and had grown too big to escape. There was a report that the monster had been seen on a road with a sheep in its mouth. Mutilated carcasses of sheep were found, said to bear the marks of the monster's teeth. Photographs were published in the newspapers, the best of which is now believed to have been faked, and a film was made, called *The Secret of the Loch*, which showed dark shapes on the surface of the water. The mystery of Nessie continues to today.

BY THE SEASIDE Coney Island in the 1930s (above), where New Yorkers went in the summer to enjoy themselves. At the British seaside, it was essential to buy saucy postcards to send to friends (right). 'I've lots of young fellows after me', the young lady claims.

whose famous 'Illuminations' became a permanent feature in 1925, had a resident population of 100 000, with 7 million visitors a year by 1931. One Bank Holiday Monday in 1937 it had over half a million, who arrived in 50 000 motor vehicles and 700 trains.

The interwar years were also the age of the holiday camp, which originated in the United States and offered 'all-in' holidays based on individual chalets and communal dining rooms. In Britain William Butlin opened the first commercial holiday camp at Skegness in 1936. He had been inspired with the idea when, on holiday in Wales, he noticed how badly the guests were treated in his boarding house. They were expected to leave after breakfast and to stay out until dinner in the evening. 'Watching these unhappy holiday-makers, I thought "What they need is a place where there are things to do when it rains".' There were 200 holiday camps in Britain by 1939, all of them offering family holidays, including food and

organised entertainment, for as little as £2-£3 a day. Meanwhile, Australians, Californians and South Africans also discovered the joys of their own superb beaches. For the increasing numbers of people who took their holidays abroad, Germany and Austria were favourite destinations right up until the outbreak of war in 1939, and Germans themselves flocked to the resorts of the Frisian Islands. Germany also led the fashion for hiking, hostelling and nude sunbathing – the *Wandervogel* with his *Lederhosen* was a familiar sight in the Europe of the 1920s, and Germany was one of the few countries to permit nude bathing.

SPEEDBOAT RIDE Society ladies enjoy a ride in a motor launch on the Potomac River in the 1920s.

SUMMER HOLIDAYS Holidaymakers waiting for trains to the south coast at Victoria station in the 1920s.

Youth hostels offered young people with little money the chance to explore the countryside. The railway companies ran 'Ramblers' Specials' and thousands of hikers would congregate at train stations in their favourite costume of berets, shorts and ankle socks, with the new steel-framed rucksacks on their backs. Thanks to cheap public transport, even the unemployed could escape from the grimness of their everyday surroundings, and many men from the industrial towns now saw green hills for the first time in their lives. Typical was John Nimlin, who recorded in 1930 how he and his unemployed friends took to walking out into the countryside around Glasgow:

'We explored Loch Lomond and the Campsie Hills, and we started camping out. One night

LIGHT REFRESHMENTS
Railway companies sold fully provisioned tea and lunch baskets for travellers. Here is tea for one, 1928.

round the camp fire we decided to start a mountaineering club: the Ptarmigan Club we called it, after the ptarmigan, a little bird that loves the mountains. Since then I've spent most of my spare time climbing . . . I believe that during the slump there were many of the despairing and the disillusioned who found a new meaning to life in the countryside.'

SPORTS AND GAMES
Huge numbers of people enjoyed spectator sports such as football, baseball and cricket. Crowds at the baseball World Series or at major British football fixtures broke all records. A crowd estimated at 150 000 turned up for the F.A. Cup Final at the new Wembley Stadium in London in 1923. Cricket enjoyed a golden age, too, producing giants such as Jack Hobbs, Wally Hammond, Herbert Sutcliffe, Leonard Hutton and the Australian Don Bradman. American sport produced its own

heroes: Knut Rockne, coach of the Notre Dame team, and Babe Ruth of the New York Yankees were better known to Americans than almost any other citizen, except the President and Charles Lindbergh.

Radio, the newspapers and cinema newsreels also enabled people to follow sports such as golf, tennis and boxing and made stars of tennis players, such as Jean Borotra (who popularised the Basque beret), Suzanne Lenglen, William Tilden and Fred Perry, or golfers, including Bobby Jones and Walter Hagen.

Heavyweight boxing, once considered disreputable, now attracted a popular following with its own heroes: the Americans Jack Dempsey, Gene Tunney and Joe Louis, the Welshman Tommy Farr, the German Max Schmelling and the Italian Primo Carnera. There were 139 999 spectators watching Tunney beat Dempsey in Philadelphia in 1926; and 40 million radio listeners heard the return bout in

SOCIAL CLIMBERS Ladies of the Turin Alpine Club refresh themselves at their first summer camp for women in the Alps, 1923.

Chicago the following year. Tunney earned nearly $2 000 000 in three years before going on to lecture on Shakespeare at Yale University.

More and more people took up swimming, tennis and golf. Tennis was one game that women could play quite freely, and women's tennis attire, with its short skirts, bandeaux and open-necked blouses, had a great influence on the liberated fashions of the 1920s. As local authorities opened public courts in parks, the sport became available to all. Golf remained, except in its home country of Scotland, a mainly middle-class game, but there were 5000 golf courses in the United States, with 2 million players dressing up in baggy plus-fours and checked stockings to play the game. Everywhere in the Anglo-Saxon world, membership of a golf or tennis club became

THE JOYS OF HIKING German women set off into the country (above) and a British poster (right) offers cheap fares to encourage hikers.

HIKE for HEALTH
SOUTHERN RAILWAY
Go-as-you-please cheap tickets get you to the country quickest

BODYLINE: 'THEY SHOULDN'T HAVE DONE THAT'

IN 1933 Patsy-Adam Smith was taken by her father to watch her first Test match. It turned out to be one of the matches in the notorious 'bodyline tour', when the English captain ordered his bowlers to aim for the batsman's body.

6 Australia was producing heroes from all walks of life, as if to remind the Mother Country that we were children no longer. We played *their* game, cricket, as if we'd invented it, and in 1930 produced "The Don", Don Bradman, a crick-

PLAYER'S CIGARETTES

D. G. BRADMAN (N. S. WALES)

eter so effective that within three years of his entering international cricket the English Test Team were ordered to stop him.

To us, Jardine was just the kind of English captain who would have sparked off the great bodyline controversy; even his clipped, Pommie voice rankled us when we heard it on the wireless.

AUSTRALIA'S HERO
Don Bradman scored 19 centuries in Test matches against England. He was knighted in 1949.

It was 1933. My father had brought me down to 'the big smoke'. I was going to watch my first Test match. When Jardine ordered his fast bowler, Harold Larwood, to aim for the body, Australians fell like men on the battlefield and all hell broke loose. Everyone jumped up, shouted, leaping over the wooden benches and making threats. All except my Dad, the quiet bushman. He sat quietly and I could scarcely hear his voice amid the uproar as he told me, "They shouldn't have done that." I then *knew* it was *wrong*. The next day the newspapers suggested we should consider seceding from England. That's the depth of feeling we had about cricket. 9

almost a badge of middle-class status, and learning the difference between golfing terms, such as a brassie and a niblick, became part of the essential equipment of the aspiring young executive.

AT HOME

People also began to develop hobbies at home, from gardening, stamp-collecting and photography to ballroom dancing, model railways and pigeon-fancying. Most of these hobbies had their own specialised illustrated magazines. People played table tennis, billiards and pool, whist, contract bridge, and commercial games such as the enormously successful Monopoly. Despite the cinema and the wireless, they continued to read, and everywhere the number of books published increased in the inter-war years. In Britain, for example, the number of titles published nearly doubled, while sales quadrupled. All the new illustrated women's magazines

THE OPEN ROAD For the less well-off, or for those who liked the wind in their hair, the motorcycle and sidecar (above), and the bicycle (left), brought freedom.

of the period, such as *Good Housekeeping, Harper's Bazaar* and *Better Homes and Gardens* in the United States, *Woman and Home* and *Woman* in Britain and *Marie Claire* in France, devoted much of their space to features on cooking and baking, knitting, dressmaking and house-furnishing, reflecting the fact that for many women shopping and home-making were themselves becoming matters of fashion and style, as well as a necessity.

In Britain in particular, there was a huge increase in the circulation of popular newspapers. In 1930 there were five dailies with circulations of over a million; by 1939 two of them had passed the 2 million mark, while two of the Sundays, the *News of the World* and *The People,* were well over 3 million by 1937. In Britain and the United States, the mass-circulation newspapers made increasing use of banner headlines and photographs, and abandoned the regular columns of the older papers for the more dramatic layout known as the 'staggered jigsaw'. They competed with one another in circulation wars, offering all kinds of inducements to regular subscribers. When the 'wars' were at their height in 1931, British papers were offering free health and life insurance; when this

TOUR DE FRANCE The cover of this 1923 French magazine shows the winner of the Tour de France, an annual event that obsesses the French as much as the Cup Final does the British.

SPORTING HEROES Frenchwoman Suzanne Lenglen (above) dominated women's tennis and, winning her last Wimbledon in 1925, lost only five games in the entire tournament. Babe Ruth (left), one of the giants of baseball, became a legend in his own lifetime.

SOMETHING FOR EVERYBODY
Magazines and children's comics had huge circulations and catered for the large increase in hobbies during the 1920s

proved to be too expensive, they started offering 'free gifts': flannel trousers for husbands, mangles for wives, and cameras, kettles, tea-sets, encyclopaedias and the works of Dickens and Shakespeare. They added gossip columns and regular comic strips, and searched for the most sensational 'exclusive' stories as well as straight news, devoting huge acreages of print and pictures to such stories as the discovery of Tutankhamun's tomb in 1923 or the alleged sightings of the Loch Ness Monster in 1933.

THE DANCING YEARS

Young people went hiking, youth-hostelling and skating – large new indoor ice rinks were being built in cities from the late 1920s on. But above all they danced. They danced in dance halls, at 'tea dances' in the afternoon, or at home to the wireless and the gramophone. The rich danced at hotels – the Savoy in London introduced the custom of dancing during meals – before going on to nightclubs or bottle parties. In the 1920s they danced to ragtime and then jazz: the Charleston, the Shimmy and the Black-bottom. The new American music shocked many of the older generation; one English clergyman wrote in 1919: 'If these up-to-date dances, described as "the latest craze", are within a hundred miles of all I hear about them, I should say that the morals of the pig-sty would be respectable in comparison.' Then, in the late 1930s, dances included the Charleston Swing, the Shag, the Suzy-Q, the Praise Allah, or Kickin' the Mule. Many

BOYS OF ALL AGES The favourite toy for boys – and their fathers – was a train set. Gauge 'O' was the most common and, as here, needed quite a large space.

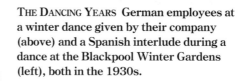

venues banned the jitterbug dance because the more spirited young women dancers revealed so much of themselves when doing it. To see how 'real' dancing should be done, they watched Vernon and Irene Castle in the 1920s, and Fred Astaire and Ginger Rogers in the 1930s.

Swing music first hit the public one night in 1935 when the clarinetist and band-leader Benny Goodman was playing at the Palomar Ballroom in Los Angeles. On the last night Goodman decided to let his band rip with the kind of loosely swinging music they liked to play in their spare time. Electrified, the ballroom came to life. Swing was born, with Goodman as its King, and soon young people everywhere were dancing to the new sound, as played by Goodman, Tommy Dorsey, Artie Shaw or Glenn Miller.

In Britain the old music hall barely survived the First World War and the advent of the cinema and the wireless. Variety theatre, and Vaudeville in the United States, however, survived in most large towns and resorts, and comedians and performers could still earn a living in them. The British variety star Gracie Fields was the most popular singer of the time, and many British and American film stars of the 1920s and 1930s began their careers on the variety stage. Weimar Berlin had its political and expressionist theatre, and its famous cabarets, which offered sharp political satire and a degree of sexual frankness not to be found elsewhere.

Traditional theatre also flourished in the larger cities, although in Britain and the United States it depended to an increasing extent on light comedies and musicals. Noël Coward and George Bernard Shaw dominated the theatre in London, along with huge one-off successes such as the musicals *Me and my Girl* and *The White Horse Inn*, the C.B. Cochran revues, and the annual production of Barrie's children's classic *Peter Pan*. In the United States, with Jerome Kern,

THE DANCING YEARS German employees at a winter dance given by their company (above) and a Spanish interlude during a dance at the Blackpool Winter Gardens (left), both in the 1930s.

George Gershwin, Cole Porter, and Rodgers and Hart on Broadway, musical comedy enjoyed its golden age.

THE CINEMA

This success was translated to the cinema screen with the spectacular musicals directed by Busby Berkeley and the timeless song-and-dance films of Fred Astaire. By the mid 1930s there were 17 000 cinemas in the United States and 5000 in Britain. Many towns which today have only one cinema had ten or more. Half the population of most European countries went to the pictures at least once a week, as did 85 million people in America. Many of the new cinemas were dramatic features of the new urban landscape, real picture palaces built in lavish 'futurist' or Babylonian styles, and often seating as many as 3000 or even 4000 people. In the United States many were air-conditioned (or refrigerated, as they were called in the 1930s). To feed demand, they each showed between

DECADENT BERLIN
A butterfly dancer from a 1927 Berlin revue, *Wann und Wo* (When and Where).

HOLLYWOOD **Stars on the stairs include Marion Davies, Douglas Fairbanks Senior and Junior, Carole Lombard, Clifton Webb, Clark Gable and Virginia Bruce.**

100 and 400 films a year. Seats were cheap. For 6d in Britain, or 25 cents in the United States (the price of a beer), cinemas offered several hours of entertainment – a main feature and a second feature, plus a newsreel, 'shorts' and at least one cartoon. With plush seats, carpeting and exotic decor, they offered an escapist degree of comfort and luxury that many of the audience could not afford in their own homes. They sold popcorn and ices, and permitted smoking – all the films of the 1920s and 30s were seen through a pall of smoke.

German, French and Russian films were much admired throughout the 1920s and 30s, but from the advent of 'talkies' at the end of the 1920s, the dominance of Hollywood as the film capital of the world was assured – and this supremacy was reinforced, in 1935, with the introduction of films in Technicolor.

FANZINE **Gossip about the lives of movie stars allowed magazines such as this one to flourish.**

Hollywood produced the most popular comedies, with stars such as Charlie Chaplin, Buster Keaton, Laurel and Hardy and the Marx Brothers. Cartoons were very popular, with characters such as Felix the Cat, and later, the creations of the cartoon genius Walt Disney. Hollywood also introduced westerns, gangster movies and musical spectaculars; and, above all, it produced the most glamour in the shape of stars such as Mary Pickford, and Marlene Dietrich, Rudolf Valentino and Douglas Fairbanks.

Hollywood reacted to the misery of the Depression by offering its audiences an escape from reality into a fantasy world of wealth and romance. This formula worked supremely well for audiences all round the world. In 1939, with war breaking out in Europe, it produced the ultimate in glamorous and romantic escapism with David Selznick's *Gone With the Wind*, starring Clark Gable and Vivien Leigh.

SUPREME STARS **Top box-office stars Leslie Howard (left) and Gary Cooper, at a dinner in 1933 in honour of Marlene Dietrich.**

DANCE Fred Astaire and Ginger Rogers in *Swing Time*, which included the song 'The Way You Look Tonight'.

The influence of Hollywood on fashion was immense. Women wore 'Garbo' coats, waved their hair like Norma Shearer, plucked their eyebrows like Marlene Dietrich, and when Ginger Rogers began to get top billing in the late 1930s, they rushed to buy girdles to emulate her narrow waist. Even men were influenced. When Clark Gable removed his shirt in the 1939 film *It Happened One Night* and revealed that he wasn't wearing an undershirt, the American textiles market dropped $8\frac{1}{4}$ per cent in one week.

The dictators of Germany, Italy and the USSR recognised the power of the cinema and made hundreds of propaganda films, but even they did not dare deprive audiences of their Hollywood movies.

BROADCASTING

Radio broadcasting began in the early 1920s and around 75 per cent of all European homes had a wireless receiver by the end of the 1930s. Relatively expensive at first, the two or three-valve wireless sets

BAND LEADERS A ticket to the Savoy Ballroom (above) for Duke Ellington (right) and his Cotton Club Orchestra. Benny Goodman with clarinet (far right). Goodman played both classical and jazz music.

dropped in price throughout the 1930s, until they were within the means of all but the poor. In Britain, broadcasting was publicly controlled from 1926 through a licensed corporation run by the high-minded John Reith; insisting on radio's responsibility to educate and uplift as well as entertain, he ensured that there were religious programmes every day of the week and that readers of the evening news dressed correctly in dinner jackets at the microphone. In the rest of Europe there were commercial stations such as Radio Luxembourg and Radio Normandie, but most broadcasting came under some degree of state control. In the USA radio broadcasting was run very much on commercial lines and advertising was an important part of this. The comedian Jack Benny, for example, was sponsored by Canada Dry, Chevrolet and General Tires, and achieved great success in 1934, under the sponsorship of Jell-O. The radio helped to reinforce family life. One of the most long-running American programmes of the 1930s was NBC's 'One Man's Family', listened to in 28 million homes every Wednesday night at 8 pm and always preceded by the announcement that it was 'dedicated to the Mothers and Fathers of the Younger Generation and to their Bewildering Offspring'. But the radio really held families together simply because it was a medium that they could enjoy together. Listening at Christmas to

LADY OF THE CAMELLIAS Elisabeth Bergner, as Marguerite Gautier, and Lothar Müthel in *Die Kameliendame*, Berlin, 1925.

Lionel Barrymore's rendering of Dickens's *A Christmas Carol* became an annual ritual for millions of American families, while most British people grew used to hearing the voice of their king after he started giving the annual Christmas message in 1932. British families heard Reith himself announce that King George's 'life is moving peacefully to a close' in 1936. Soon after, they heard Edward VIII announce his abdication, and in 1939 they heard the Prime Minister announce that the country was at war. Because it was a mass medium

SWING Tommy Dorsey (above) set the swing beat with his trombone.

THE ADVENT OF 'TALKIES'

The first true sound film, made in Germany in 1925, was *The Little Match Girl*, based on the story by Hans Andersen. However, the sound quality was poor and the film was taken off after only two days. The first successful sound film was *The Jazz Singer*, starring Al Jolson, which appeared in 1927. Its phenomenal success spelt the end for silent pictures and the careers of many silent movie actors and actresses, whose voices were found to be less attractive than their features.

TERROR ON THE AIRWAVES

NOTHING illustrated the power of radio over its listeners better than the Orson Welles dramatisation in 1938 of *The War of the Worlds* by H.G. Wells.

On the evening of Sunday, October 30, 1938, millions of people were listening to the radio. Those listening to dance music on the CBS channel had their programme interrupted by news bulletins from the New Jersey town of Grovers Mill, where, it was claimed, a strange metallic cylinder had been found. At 8.12 pm the announcer broke into the programme to say:

'Just a minute! Something's happening! Ladies and gentlemen, this is terrific. The end of the thing is beginning to flake off! The top is beginning to rotate like a screw!'

Seconds later, with excited crowd noises in the background, the announcer was sobbing:

'Good heavens, something's wriggling out of the shadow like a gray snake. Now it's another one, and another! They look like tentacles to me. There, I can see, the thing's body. It's large as a bear and it glistens like wet leather. But that face. It . . . it's indescribable. I can hardly force myself to keep looking at it. The eyes are black and gleam like a serpent.'

Soon policemen are reported to be advancing on the strange object, but the creatures turned a heat-ray on them and terrible screams were heard as they are burned to cinders. Then another announcer informed the listening audience:

'Incredible as it may seem . . . those strange beings who landed in the Jersey farmlands tonight are the vanguard of an invading army from the planet Mars.'

He revealed that martial law had been declared and the President had

announced a national emergency. The Army Air Corps was wiped out. Then an operator announced jerkily:

'Warning! Poisonous black smoke pouring in from Jersey marshes . . . Gas masks useless. Urge population to move into open spaces . . . automobiles use routes 7, 23, 24 . . . Avoid congested areas. Smoke now spreading over Raymond Boulevard.'

Then came the announcement that Martian cylinders were falling all over the country – 'One outside Buffalo, one in Chicago, St Louis. . . .'

Those who had heard the beginning of the programme at 8pm had been told that what they were about to hear was a dramatic fiction. That message was repeated at intervals throughout the broadcast. But an estimated 1.7 million listeners were convinced that they had tuned in to

REHEARSALS Orson Welles, with hands upraised, guides a rehearsal at the 'Mercury Theatre of the Air'.

genuine news bulletins, and by 8.30 pm hundreds of thousands of them had taken to the streets from Maine to California, screaming in panic. Roads in New Jersey were choked with mobs of sobbing people. Churches were packed with weeping families, convinced the end of the world had come, and in some towns there was rioting and looting.

By the end of the programme, the CBS studios had been surrounded by police. During the next two days the network made regular announcements to assure listeners that the broadcast had been fictitious.

SORRY ABOUT THAT After the dramatic broadcast Welles was lucky to escape prosecution.

music in the evening. Sports commentaries covered all the major events. From January 1934 children all over the United States were listening to *The Lone Ranger*, and it was the United States which developed the radio serial (which came to be known as 'soap opera' because of its advertising sponsorship).

In the 1930s a typical American newspaper listing of children's programmes might be:

5.15	WTIC	1040	Tom Mix
	WEAF	660	Story Man
5.30	WTIC	1040	Jack Armstrong
	WJZ	760	Singing Lady
5.45	WJZ	760	Little Orphan Annie
6.0	WOR	710	Uncle Don.

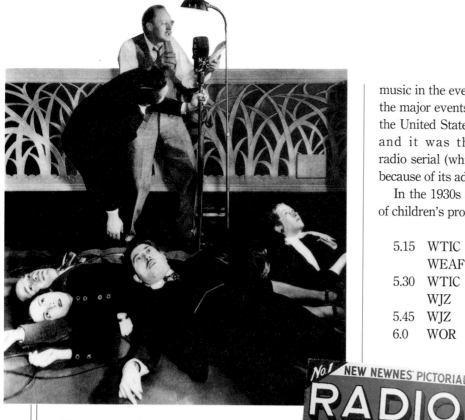

DRAMA ON THE AIR Murder victims on the studio floor during an NBC 'Lights Out' radio show (above). Radio magazines (right) fed readers' interest in the stars.

accessible to all, radio also served to reduce regional differences; for example, although few people actually spoke like the BBC's announcers, radio gradually reduced the wider extremes of dialect in the country.

The broadcasting formula was similar in most countries: light music and women's programmes during the day; children's programmes in the late afternoon; comedy, drama and classical and dance

As well as having its own children's programmes, Britain (and Europe) offered more serious drama. When the BBC began broadcasting serial episodes of classic novels such as *Les Miserables* and *The Count of Monte Cristo* on Sunday evening in the late 1930s, clergymen complained of empty churches at Evensong; and Wednesday night's *Band Wagon* programme was so popular that receipts in cinemas and theatres around the country dropped sharply. Everywhere in the world people felt the power of a medium which worked in the theatre of the imagination.

CHORUS LINE Radio City Music Hall, New York, featured the Rockettes. This is the 1937 line-up.

MIND, BODY AND SPIRIT

Old diseases were being conquered and bodies grew healthier,

thanks mainly to improved diet and sanitation. Traditional religion

declined but the need for something to believe in was channelled in new

directions. Elementary education was available to all,

but remained deeply conservative. Universities were still places

for a privileged few.

HEALTH AND EDUCATION

Better housing and public sanitation had more to do with improved public

health than medical science. And efforts were being made to

safeguard the health of children at school

THE PERIOD between the wars began with one of the severest holocausts of disease ever encountered, the influenza epidemic of 1918-19. It killed some 27 million people worldwide, many more than the First World War itself, including many young men who had escaped death in battle. More than 8 million people died in India alone. Australian and New Zealand soldiers, perhaps because of low levels of immunity, were particularly badly affected. In Britain there were 200 000 deaths; in Germany, where physical resistance had been weakened by food shortages due to the Allied blockade, at least twice that number died. Whole households, sometimes entire streets, were affected, with all family members dangerously ill in bed at the same time.

That apart, the overall picture from 1918 to 1939 was one of steady improvement in the health of the population, with a rising life expectancy and a striking decrease in child mortality. The life expectancy of a child born in 1900 was 48 years; in 1935 it was 60 years. Also, the fact that children were much more likely to survive infancy was one of the reasons for people opting for smaller families. Major killer diseases, such as tuberculosis, typhoid and pneumonia, were either eliminated or beginning to come under control, and there was a noticeable increase in the average height and weight of children.

These improvements were due in large part to improved housing – especially the large-scale clearance of overcrowded and insanitary urban slums

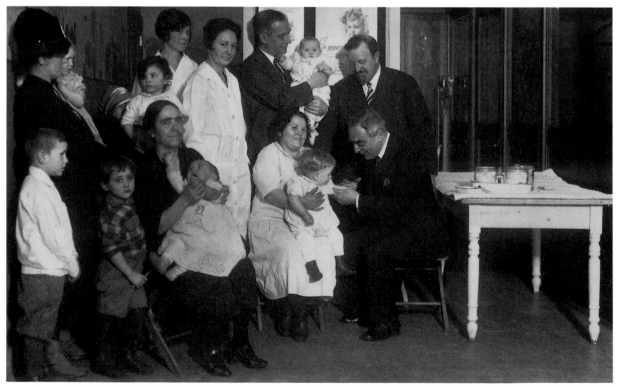

FIGHTING DISEASE A New York doctor inoculates a child against diphtheria in 1929.

SIR ALEXANDER FLEMING AND THE DISCOVERY OF PENICILLIN

MIRACLE WORKER Sir Alexander Fleming (above) discovered penicillin in his laboratory in 1928. A culture plate (right) developed a mould which Fleming found could be used to treat infections.

DR ALEXANDER FLEMING discovered penicillin at St Mary's Hospital, Paddington, in 1928. Returning from holiday, he saw a pile of culture plates which he had left behind in a shady corner of the laboratory. On the point of sending them for cleaning, he paused to use them to demonstrate something to one of his students, and then noticed that on one of the plates there was an absence of staphylococcal growth in the vicinity of the mould that had formed on it.

His analysis of the mould and its effects was published in 1929 but attracted little attention at the time. Fleming's accidental discovery had prepared the way for the antibiotic treatment of infectious diseases. Purified penicillin did not come into general use until 1941, and this was eventually recognised in 1945, when Fleming shared the Nobel prize for Physiology with Ernst Boris Chain and Howard Walter Florey, who had done important work in further isolating, purifying and mass-producing penicillin. But throughout the inter-war years, bacterial infection of accidental wounds, or in association with surgery, remained a major health hazard, although the problem had been greatly alleviated by improved hygiene and antiseptic procedures in surgeries. It was the Second World War, in which penicillin saved countless lives, that stimulated a significant advance in this area.

– and to better diet and hygiene, as well as safer, more abundant water supplies. Efficient public sewerage systems made typhoid a relatively rare disease in North America and Western Europe. Although there were epidemics of typhoid in the South of England in 1936 and 1937, there were no major outbreaks in France after 1929. They were also due to advances in medical knowledge and skills.

Preventive medicine was not well developed, and doctors still spent much of their time trying to cure or mitigate illnesses that could often have been prevented, but there were a few serious attempts made to try to make public health a matter of national concern. In France, for example, nurses were sent to visit private houses as part of the fight against tuberculosis, and from 1930 there was a compulsory premarital medical examination to detect possible communicable diseases.

There was much greater understanding of nutritional science and of the importance of vitamins, proteins and minerals in the diet and of their connection with deficiency diseases. However, little was done by governments before the late 1930s to ensure that the poor received the kind of nutrition recommended by the experts. Despite the overall picture of improving health, large numbers of those

SUMMER CAMP Boys at the Eagle Hill health camp, Washington DC, 1938.

CHILDREN'S HEALTH CAMP

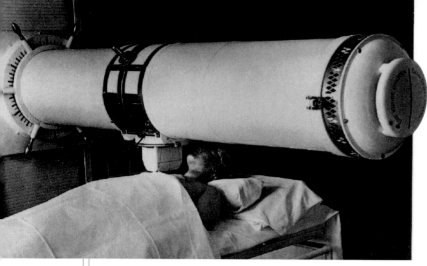

WEAPONS AGAINST TB Ray-treatment with a 'cannon', carried out at a tuberculosis clinic near Brandenburg in Germany, 1930.

affected by unemployment in the 1930s (perhaps a tenth of the population) suffered from malnutrition, and especially from lack of protein and vitamins in the diet. From 1934 about half the children in British elementary schools were being provided with one-third of a pint of milk daily, either free or at low cost and in 1939 health departments began to give cod-liver oil and iron and vitamin supplements to mothers and small children who were clearly malnourished.

Public awareness of the importance of a balanced diet was spread to some extent through education, but probably even more through discussion in news-papers and women's magazines. Vitamins, though not well understood chemically, became positively fashionable, and led to the opening of large numbers of health food shops selling exotic nuts, dried fruits, herbal teas and cereals. One special bread was advertised in Britain with the words. 'The secret of its nourishment is the wonderful vitamine it contains: without this, health cannot be maintained.'

Diet apart, the newspapers paid little attention to preventive medicine, but it frequently featured dramatic new developments in medical treatments. From the 1920s, insulin brought relief to diabetics, and in the 1930s pneumonia was treated with sulphonomides and diphtheria by immunisation of children. X-ray treatment began to be used success-fully for the treatment of some cancers. X-ray machines were also used in the footwear departments of the bigger stores to ensure a good fit, but the danger of this exposure was not appreciated at the time.

THE MEDICAL PROFESSION: A CITADEL UNDER SIEGE

A.J. CRONIN (1896–1981) was a doctor and novelist whose disillusionment with medical practice in the 1930s spurred him to write *The Citadel*.

Although fiction, its disturbing insights made it an immediate and much-discussed bestseller. It was also made into a film. Here, the hero, Andrew Manson, confronts the medical council's charge of infamous professional conduct.

❛ If they were going to strike him off, let him give them cause to do so. He rushed on: "I've listened to the pleading that's been going on today on my behalf and all the time I've been asking myself what harm I've done. I don't want to work with quacks. I don't believe in bogus remedies . . . I know I'm speaking more strongly than I should, but I can't help it. We're not nearly liberal enough. If we go on trying to make out that everything's wrong outside the profession and everything is right within, it means the death of scientific progress. We'll just turn into a tight little trade protection society. It's high time we started putting our own house in order, and I don't mean the superficial things either . . . When I qualified I was more of a menace to society than anything else. All I knew was the names of a few diseases and the drugs I was supposed to give for them. I couldn't even lock a pair of midwifery forceps . . . But how many doctors do learn anything beyond the ordinary rudiments they pick up in practice. They haven't got time, poor devils, they're rushed off their feet. That's where our whole organisation is rotten . . . There ought to be compul-sory post-graduate classes. There ought to be a great attempt to bring science into the front line, to do away with the old bottle-of-medicine idea, give every practitioner a chance to study, to co-operate in research . . . The whole profession is far too intolerant and smug . . . We never think of advancing, altering our system. We say we'll do things and we don't. For years we've been bleating about the sweated conditions under which our nurses work, the wretched pittances we pay them. Well? They're still being sweated, still paid their pittances. That's just an example. . . . " ❜

THE RIGHT START A school prefect distributes spoonfuls of cod-liver oil to pupils in a British school in the late 1920s. At a London school in 1936 (right) milk was distributed to the pupils each day. It cost one halfpenny for one-third of a pint.

Tuberculosis remained a problem. It was controlled by the provision of more sanatoriums, especially in France, and, from the early 1920s, by the pasteurisation of milk. In Germany, for example, the number of deaths from TB almost halved between 1913 and 1928, but in 1924 the disease was still sufficiently in people's minds for the German writer Thomas Mann to set his great symbolic novel, *The Magic Mountain,* in a mountain sanatorium where the inmates, with the high colour and nervous temperament characteristic of tuberculosis, spend their days discussing philosophy and the problems of the age. Venereal diseases, though rarely discussed in public, took a heavy toll of life. In France alone, 140 000 people died from syphilis every year.

THE SPREAD OF DISEASE

As older infectious diseases came under control, heart disease and cancer became commoner causes of death. Polio or infantile paralysis was greatly feared, too. American parents who could afford to do so sent their children away to summer camp to escape the risk of polio, and when it struck they stayed away from cinemas and other public places and often wore gauze masks whenever they went outdoors. The high incidence and mortality rate of polio in National Socialist Germany was blamed on the large numbers of open-air swimming pools built by the Hitler Youth movement which failed to provide adequate safeguards against the spread of infection.

DOCTORS AND HOSPITALS

Ironically, the terrible wounds sustained in the First World War had given surgeons experience that was to be valuable in peacetime. Techniques of brain and lung surgery greatly improved, along with the provision of more sophisticated types of artificial limbs. The war also introduced the large-scale adoption of blood transfusion. By the late 1930s blood donors were being registered and classified according to the recently discovered blood groups. Dentists were beginning to use cocaine in a primitive form, although it was not always available. High-speed drills had not yet been developed so a visit to the dentist was still an uncomfortable and unpleasant experience. In the operating theatre chloroform was replacing ether, but although

BOTTLED GOODNESS
Cod-liver oil, Bovril and fruit salts from the 1920s, taken to promote good health.

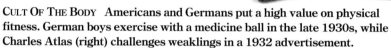

CULT OF THE BODY Americans and Germans put a high value on physical fitness. German boys exercise with a medicine ball in the late 1930s, while Charles Atlas (right) challenges weaklings in a 1932 advertisement.

antiseptic surgery was now firmly established, much treatment was still carried out without anaesthesia. By 1939 in Britain, the National Insurance system gave almost 20 million workers, but not their families, a free general practitioner service and sickness benefit paid out by trade unions and benefit clubs. Workers' families, the self-employed and most of the middle class had to depend on private insurance schemes and sickness clubs. There were some 3000 hospitals in the country, with 250 000 beds. Working people could obtain free treatment in them by paying 3d per week

---

A NOVEL CURE

One of the health fads of the 1920s was for the teachings of the French pharmacist Dr Emile Coué (1857–1926), who developed a form of psychotherapy. Its best-known feature was the frequent repetition of the words: 'Every day, and in every way, I am getting better and better.' Before long, he had a wide following in Britain and the United States as well as in France. One of his successes was to cure several passengers on the liner *Majestic* of seasickness during a particularly rough Atlantic crossing. He started by training the stewardesses in his method.

---

into a hospital fund and many large companies covered their employees for hospital treatment by making an annual bulk payment on their behalf. 'Free' hospitals provided for the very poor who could not afford the necessary contributions. However, the National Insurance system did not include ophthalmic care, maternity services or dental treatment. There was a massive problem of decayed teeth, especially among the poor, and it was quite usual for working-class people to have false teeth – or no teeth – in their later years. Where spectacles were needed, many working-class people resorted to Woolworth, which offered facilities for 'do-it-yourself' eye tests for a few pence. Stores such as Harrods sent sample ranges of spectacles to better-off customers living in the country so that they could select lenses that suited them.

In France, where a ministry of public health was established in 1930, the number of doctors increased from 20 000 to 35 000. In Weimar Germany the situation was similar. A real effort was made to improve public health provision. The number of doctors almost doubled between 1918 and 1930, and the number of hospital beds increased by 50 per cent. One darker feature of the time in Germany, however, was the widespread interest in eugenics – the prevention and eradication by means of sterilisation of supposedly congenital diseases, physical and

THE FLYING DOCTORS OF AUSTRALIA

EVER SINCE the settlers moved out into the remoter parts of Australia they had been faced with the problem of how to obtain emergency medical services. The scattered homesteads simply could not support the services of a doctor, let alone a fully equipped surgery, and the distances were such that a patient might well not survive the drive to the nearest hospital. In 1917 Clifford Peel, a young medical student from Victoria, suggested that flying ambulances were the answer, but there remained the problem of how such help could be summoned to places unconnected by telephone. The solution came in 1928 when Alfred Traeger, an electrical engineer, designed a simple to use, inexpensive radio transceiver, with a range of about 300 miles (480 km). The practicability of the flying ambulance had been demonstrated in 1927 when Dr George Simpson flew nearly 1243 miles (2000 km) from Cloncurry in Queensland to pick up a miner with a broken pelvis and bring him back for treatment.

The combination of the radio and aeroplane made possible the flying-doctor service, which was established

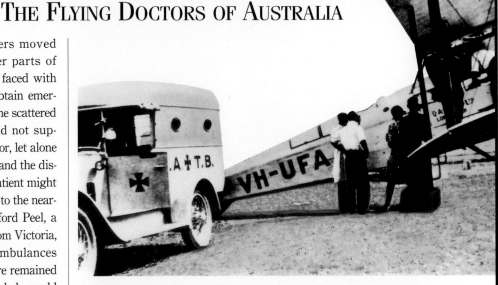

AIR AMBULANCE The Australian flying doctor service was set up in Queensland in 1928 to serve the far-flung communities of the continent.

at Cloncurry in May 1928 with a Qantas De Havilland DH50 mail plane carrying Dr Vincent Welch and a pilot. During the first year Dr Welch flew 19 885 miles (32 000 km) and attended 255 patients. In 1931 Dr Allan Vickers, flew over 1243 miles (2000 km) in a vain attempt to save the life of a hotel-keeper injured by the explosion of a kerosene refrigerator, but the flight was not entirely wasted because on the return trip he was able to carry poliomyelitis serum that saved a boy from lifelong paralysis.

Before long the flying doctors were serving the outlying settlements of the whole continent. Doctors could sometimes prescribe by radio, without attending personally. As one doctor put it, they were called on to prescribe 'for babies with gastritis, toddlers with measles and whooping cough, children with trachoma or sprained ankles, a lad badly burnt, a woman bitten by a red-backed spider, an old bushman in his billabong camp crippled with sciatica – anything in the seven ages of man'.

---

mental deficiencies and antisocial tendencies – even among liberal and socialist thinkers.

In the United States, however, there was no public provision of health care and little medical insurance before 1933 when Roosevelt became president.

TRAVEL SICKNESS
An Italian magazine advertisement offers a remedy for tummy trouble, 1932.

Hospital treatment was relatively cheap, but before the mid-1930s most people still preferred to have their illnesses at home. American family doctors, like their counterparts in Europe, still thought it a normal part of their job to call on their patients. They were among the first people to use the motor car as a professional aid rather than as a leisure vehicle.

Doctors still had a strong personal relationship with the families they treated, often over several generations. In some areas they presented their bills annually. In some parts of France they presented them only when the patient died. Only specialists, increasingly numerous from the 1930s onwards, charged immediately for their services, a practice that was regarded by traditional family doctors as deplorably commercial.

BEDTIME DRINKS Horlicks Malted Milk first appeared in the 1880s in the USA, while Ovaltine first appeared in Britain in 1909.

By the mid 1930s more people were going to hospitals and growing used to the idea of them as places to be born and to die, whereas most Victorians had begun and ended their lives at home. However, hospital treatment was not well co-ordinated. Some hospitals were run by local authorities; some, such as the great teaching hospitals, were independent and supported by charitable foundations and voluntary subscriptions. Others were entirely private and run on commercial lines. The quality of hospitals varied enormously from place to place. Some were still Victorian – or even medieval-like – institutions which probably managed to kill just as many people as they cured. But the newer ones, with their trained staff and bright, airy wards, hygienic conditions, and use of the new scientific equipment, were beginning to look very much like the hospitals of today.

The general preoccupation with health prevalent at the time was much exploited by advertisers. Horlicks introduced the public to the condition known as 'Night Starvation' and vowed that its malted milk was an infallible aid to sound sleep. Manufacturers of health salts promised 'Inner Cleanliness'. Bovril offered associations with the great men of the past: 'Napoleon's Secret. The secret of Napoleon's success was his immense vitality. The same is true of most great men – Julius Caesar, Michelangelo, Gladstone, Cecil Rhodes – they were successful because they were never tired. Don't get tired, drink Bovril.'

Much more dangerously, benzedrine was heavily advertised in the 1930s as a 'confidence drug', which was added to cocktails and freely available from chemists' shops until its connection with an increasing number of suicides was noticed by

MARIE STOPES, BIRTH-CONTROL PIONEER

CONTRACEPTION IN one form or another had been practised since the dawn of time. By the end of the 19th century mechanical forms of contraception – the sheath and the cap – were available. However, contraception was opposed by the Church and public discussion of it frowned upon.

MARRIED LOVE Campaigner Dr Marie Stopes marries Humphrey Roe, 1926.

Some pioneers believed that education in the use of contraception was essential for the sexual liberty and health of women, and the only answer to the evils of back-street abortion.

The leader of this movement in Britain was Dr Marie Stopes (1880-1958, a doctor of science, not medicine). In 1922 she hired the Queen's Hall in London to advocate her views, which were condemned by both the Catholic and Anglican clergy. Some doctors also opposed her views. She pointed out that they would often tell a woman that having another child would mean death, but never told her

how to avoid having children, except by abstinence. Recognising that working-class women were most in need of advice, she opened her first clinic in London in 1921. In the first three months she had 20 000 requests for abortions from women who could not face another pregnancy; instead, she advised the use of contraceptives.

Marie Stopes fought on against all opposition. The profits of her highly successful books, *Married Love* and *Wise Parenthood* published in 1918, were ploughed into her campaign. By the end of the 1920s the battle was essentially won, particularly after she recommended that contraceptive devices should only be fitted to married women. In 1939 the Family Planning Association was founded.

CLEANLINESS AND GODLINESS Hands and fingernails are inspected by fellow pupils, Louisville, USA, *c.*1920.

coroners and it was put on the dangerous drugs list. The advertising of patent medicines had grown enormously and was largely uncontrolled. One British Sunday newspaper in 1938 carried advertisements in a single issue for 'cures' for epilepsy, varicose veins, piles, eczema, rheumatism, neuritis, hayfever, asthma, malaria, influenza, headaches, depression, insomnia, indigestion, constipation and impure blood. In the United States, legislation was passed in 1935 to prohibit the advertisement of 'cures' for serious disorders such as cancer, blindness and epilepsy. A similar Parliamentary Bill was introduced in Britain in 1936, but failed to pass its second Commons reading as it came up on a day when most members had gone to see the Grand National steeplechase.

There was still room for improvement in the health of the public. During an Army recruiting drive in Britain in 1935 it was found that 62 per cent of applicants failed to reach the relatively low standard of physique required. By 1940, when young conscripts from the population as a whole were being examined for military service, the proportion of those unfit had fallen to under one-third, compared with almost two-thirds in the First World War. In this respect young Germans and Americans of the late 1930s, with a more nourishing diet and more attention paid to sport and physical fitness, were probably in better condition.

THE EDUCATIONAL DIVIDE

In the interwar years all the countries of North America, Western Europe, Australia, New Zealand and South Africa provided free schooling to some extent, but education everywhere divided people according to wealth or academic talent. In Britain from 1918 there was free and compulsory education for all children up to the age of 14. By 1939 British state education was a two-tier system offering primary education up to the age of 11 or 12, followed by secondary education either at grammar schools, for those with higher academic scores, or at 'modern' schools, which specialised in technical subjects for boys and domestic science for girls. Most of the grammar schools were fee-paying, but offered free places for which pupils were examined at 11; many of them imitated the uniforms and rituals of the independent public schools. The British educationalist Robin Pedley went from an elementary school to Richmond Grammar School between the wars and found the experience something of a shock:

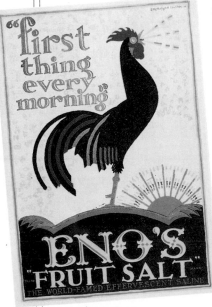

A FRESH START
1925 Punch advertisement for Enos fruit salts by McKnight Kauffer.

131

UNWILLINGLY TO SCHOOL Unenthusiastic children contemplate a school-registration poster, New York, 1923.

'I entered a different world. For the first time I wore a tailored grey suit, stiff collar, and school cap. I felt a guilty turncoat when the elementary-school children of the town chanted "Grammar, grammar matchstalks" derisively at us as we walked long-trousered through the cobbled streets. Inside the school too, my life was turned upside down. It was not only that for the first time I encountered such subjects as Latin and French, physics and chemistry, algebra and geometry; I had expected that. What amazed me was the elaborate apparatus devised to get boys to do what the staff wanted. Essays and tests all reaped their quotas of marks, religiously added up and announced at half-term and end of term. There were colours for doing well at rugger and cricket; points for one's house, prizes for this, lines, or even the cane, for that.'

Only about 6 per cent of children attended the public schools themselves, which nevertheless provided a quarter of all university students and the overwhelming majority of Oxford and Cambridge graduates. Former pupils of a handful of the great public schools, such as Eton, Harrow, Winchester and Westminster, filled most of the top jobs in the country. Most of the public schools, as Robert Graves put it, 'continued to give their pupils heavy Victorian food to eat and heavy Victorian clothes and hats to wear; teach them little but the Classics, mathematics,

MOVING BOOKS A travelling library provided by the local council in 1930s England.

ONE-ROOM SCHOOL   Oakdale school, Tennessee, 1934. The pupils' fathers work for the Tennessee Valley Authority.

Scripture, and a little French; make crimes of small offences; and rout them out of bed early with the clang of the school bell for long and listless prayers'.

France was unique in its highly centralised system of public education, which determined what was taught in schools, right down to the smallest detail. Elementary schooling was free and compulsory. Secondary schools charged fees and were graded into *écoles* and *lycées*; the latter, designed to produce the country's administrative elite, placed a heavy emphasis on classical studies. In Weimar Germany there was an attempt to set up a comprehensive state education system, but a divided system not unlike the British one persisted. From elementary schools that were common to all, pupils moved on to one of the independent church schools; or to a *Gymnasium* (high school) for the better-off or more academic; or to a technical school.

The United States had comprehensive education for all but the small minority who attended private schools such as Groton or the Choate School or Miss Porter's, or the country's numerous military schools. Only half of all American children attending elementary school went on to high school – far fewer than now – and there were 150 000 schools in country areas with only one teacher, providing the very basic education that was all that millions of children had in those years.

AT SCHOOL

Reformers in Weimar Germany tried to introduce a more child-centred form of education to the traditional one. The theories of Froebel and Madame Montessori had some influence on the more progressive European schools; and there were experimental schools in Britain, such as Dartington Hall and the permissively run schools founded by pioneers such as A.S. Neill

---

SCHOOL DONKEYS

In the Transvaal, South Africa, the government provided donkeys to improve school attendance in country districts. The donkeys were stamped for identification and the scheme was still operative in the 1940s. Sometimes, however, things went awry, as school logbooks reveal. 'Piet was late for school because the donkey could not be found.' 'John was absent because the donkey died.'

EYEWITNESS

AN ENGLISH VILLAGE SCHOOL

THE HEADMISTRESS of the village school in Akenfield, Suffolk, kept a logbook in which major events in the life of the school were recorded. Here is the log for 1928.

❛ Diphtheria has broken out in the village.

A picture *Youth* for hanging on the wall has been received from the East Suffolk Education Committee.

The Inspector called and watched Drawing, Needlework, Singing and Country Dancing.

Two children have died from diphtheria, and Dr Stocks has taken swabs from all the scholars. The school has been closed.

The water supply has been tested and it has been suggested that the children bring their own cups in future, instead of using the one enamel mug by the tap.

On Armistice Day the scholars "listened-in" to the Cenotaph Service by the kindness of Mr Bulmer, who lent them his portable wireless set.

Mary Ruth Bridge has been appointed Pupil-Teacher at a salary of £10 the first year, £12 the second year and £20 the third year. She is 15 years of age.

55 children on the register. ❜

and Bertrand Russell. Australia, with many children living in very small, isolated communities, developed special expertise in one-teacher, one-room 'bush schools', for which it earned international recognition. It also developed correspondence education, supplemented by radio from the early 1930s, at all levels from primary to university. But the teaching methods in most schools everywhere were still very conservative, the children sitting in orderly rows facing the teacher and the blackboard and doing much of their learning by rote. Young children in British primary schools wrote their exercises on slates; the older ones dipped their pens in inkwells fitted into the desks, using the copperplate handwriting they had learned from copybooks. The British writer Laurie Lee went to a country school in the early 1920s:

'Our village school was small and crowded, but in the end I relished it. It had a lively reek of steaming life: boys' boots, girls' hair, stoves and sweat, blue ink, white chalk and shavings. We learnt nothing abstract or tenuous there – just simple patterns of facts and letters, portable tricks of calculation, not more than was needed to measure a shed, write out a bill, read a swine-disease warning. Through the dead hours of the morning, through the long afternoons, we chanted away at tables. Passers-by could hear our rising voices in our bottled-up room on the bank: "Twelve-inches-one-foot. Three-feet-make-a-yard. Fourteen-pounds-make-a-stone. Eight-stone-a-hundredweight." We absorbed these figures as primal truths declared by some ultimate power.'

William Manchester describes his American schoolboy of the early 1930s. His day began with a pledge of allegiance to the flag:

'To school he also brought a Masterpiece tablet, bearing on its cover a blurry reproduction of a

THEM AND US Schoolboys from different backgrounds wait outside Lord's Cricket Ground during the Eton versus Harrow match, 1937.

HIGH SERIOUSNESS German students and teachers at a *Gymnasium* in Berlin in 1930.

great painting; in it he laboriously copied assignments with a big, circular Palmer Penmanship script. Seats in the classroom were frequently arranged alphabetically. The walls of at least one room would be decorated with the ruins of Pompeii or a bust of Caesar.'

Discipline in most schools was strict and rigorously enforced for what was believed to be the good of the child. One American textbook summed up the typical view of both teachers and parents:

'The child who has not learned obedience is handicapped for life. If he does not obey at home, he is not likely to observe the laws of the state, even though he helps elect the men who make them. Boys and girls who study our Government will quickly discover that obedience to authority is as necessary in a government by the people as in a monarchy.'

UNIVERSITY LIFE

Many new universities were founded between the wars, but only a small minority of the population had a university education: in Britain in 1938 only 2 per cent of all 19-year-olds were still receiving full-time education. For the wealthy minority who could attend Cambridge or Oxford, the older German universities or America's Ivy League colleges at their own or their parents' expense, their university years were a time of privilege and leisure. Oxford and Cambridge undergraduates in the frivolous 1920s had their own fashions in dress, whether for yellow hunting waistcoats, suede shoes,

THE BEST DAYS Stories of public school life were popular in Britain. Billy Bunter and friends at Greyfriars (left). Schoolboy anecdotes (right) by novelist Ian Hay.

HIGH LIFE IN OXFORD

THE BRITISH WRITER Evelyn Waugh recalled his days at Oxford in more than one novel. He opened his 1928 novel *Decline and Fall* with a scene set in the imaginary college of Scone, where two senior dons, Mr Sniggs and Mr Postlewaithe, are listening to the sounds of revelry from some of the richer young undergraduates:

❛ From the rooms of Sir Alistair Digby-Vaine-Trumpington, two staircases away, came a confused roaring and breaking of glass. They alone of the senior members of Scone were at home that evening, for it was the annual dinner of the Bollinger Club . . .

It is not accurate to call this an annual event, because quite often the club is suspended for some years after each meeting. There is this tradition behind the Bollinger; it numbers kings among its past members. At the last dinner, three years ago, a fox had been brought in a cage and stoned to death with champagne bottles. What an evening that had been! This was the first meeting since then, and from all over Europe old members had rallied for the occasion. For two days they had been pouring into Oxford . . .

"The fines!" said Mr Sniggs, gently rubbing his pipe along the side of his nose. "Oh, my! the fines there'll be after this evening!"

There is some highly prized port in the senior common room cellars that is only brought up when the College fines have reached £50. ❜

velveteen trousers or the wide trousers known as 'Oxford bags', in addition to the huge range of scarves and blazers of the colleges and clubs. As well as exclusive dining societies and lavish private entertaining in college rooms, they delighted in forming eccentric clubs, such as Cambridge's University Pavement Club, which spent an hour at midday sitting on the pavement of King's Parade, passing the time with tiddlywinks or marbles, reading or knitting; or the Oxford Railway Club, which specialised in dining and drinking on night trains in full evening dress; or the climbing clubs of both universities, whose members climbed the most challenging of Gothic roofs and spires at night, causing considerable damage to the fabric. Only in the early 1930s did Oxford and Cambridge men begin to sober up and, in many cases, turn to left-wing politics.

Ivy League colleges had their exclusive clubs too, but American students also favoured fraternity rituals, raccoon-skin coats, lettered sweaters, sports cars, college football, and, in the Prohibition years, jazz, the hip-flask and wild drinking parties. The love of ritual and exclusiveness was particularly strong at the old German universities, such as Bonn, Freiburg, Gottingen and Heidelberg, with their medieval traditions and their duelling fraternities. Despite the fact that the Nazis banned such duelling, it continued at Heidelberg, using rapiers rather than the traditional sabre. After 1933 all education in Germany fell into the hands of the Nazis, and although they did not often intervene directly in the classroom, they ensured that children of all ages were indoctrinated with National Socialist theory and Führer-worship. They replaced existing textbooks in subjects like history and biology with versions of their own, reduced religious instruction and placed a very high emphasis on sport and physical education.

A MATTER OF HONOUR
Students in Germany prepare for a duel in the 1930s. The eyes and the upper part of the body are protected.

RELIGION IN AN AGE OF UNCERTAINTY

As traditional faith weakened, the religious impulse

sometimes flowed towards faith in Karl Marx or the doctrines

of extreme nationalism.

DURING the postwar years there was a decline in orthodox religious belief and in church membership and attendance – all part of the disillusion of the times. In the minds of ex-soldiers particularly, churches were associated with the mood of bellicose patriotism on the home front that they had come to loathe and despise. This cynicism was also due in part to the challenge to religion from scientific doctrines such as relativity and Darwinian theory. It was particularly striking among the Protestant churches of Europe and in large urban centres, where new ways of spending Sunday competed with old habits of churchgoing. For many, Sunday as a day of rest and worship had given way to Sunday as part of the weekend leisure break, now that most people had Saturday afternoons off. For an increasing number of families it was the day for a round of golf or a drive into the country. The English writer J.B. Priestley noticed the change when he was travelling around the country in 1933 and visited a nonconformist chapel in Birmingham:

'The chief difference in the congregation was that there were fewer young people in it, and especially young men. If there were any boys present, they escaped my eye. There were a few little girls, a sprinkling of older girls and young women, and all the

AMERICAN SUNDAY Worshippers leaving the Methodist church at Linworth, Ohio, in the 1930s.

137

A NEW RELIGION? **A cross surrounded by fire in Dusseldorf, 1933 – Nazis commemorate the death of a German killed by the French in 1923 (left). The Church of St Lawrence, Nuremburg, in 1933 (above), dressed for (Nazi) Party Day celebrations.**

one of the two official Christian denominations until as late as 1937. Church leaders still pronounced on matters of public morality, mainly taking a conservative line on such issues as divorce, birth control and Sunday drinking laws, and condemning alcohol, gambling and even bridge-playing. In Britain they played a crucial part in forcing the abdication of King Edward VIII because the woman he wanted to marry was twice-divorced. Germany of the 1930s was divided into those who preached extreme nationalism and anti-Semitism and those who opposed Nazism. In the United States, Father Coughlin, 'the Radio Priest', peddled right-wing views and racial hatred to a radio audience estimated at 45 million on his 'Golden Hour of the Little Flower'.

rest of the congregation and the choir were middle-aged. But I suppose that in my chapel-going days, there would actually have been twice the number of people at this service.'

The decline was less marked in the United States, and in smaller country communities. Among Catholics, the church and the priest remained a vital centre of local life. Churchgoing was still, for many, one of the badges of respectable middle-class life, and most people still went to church for christenings, weddings and funerals, though they might not attend at any other time. Religion still played an important part in the official life of the country; legislatures and schools began their proceedings with prayer; there were chapels in prisons and chaplains attached to the armed forces; the German army maintained its rule that every soldier must belong to

Some of the younger clergy, especially those who had seen service as army chaplains, made serious attempts to bring the Church into line with changing social needs; others tried to make churchgoing 'brighter' to compete with the attractions of the secular world. Churches began to offer more non-religious activities such as amateur theatricals, whist drives and bring-and-buy sales. But, as the American historian Frederick Allen noted: 'Something spiritual had gone out of the churches – a sense of certainty that theirs was the way to salvation.'

There were plenty of signs that the religious impulse itself – the

ABDICATION CRISIS
The twice-divorced Mrs Wallis Simpson and the former King Edward VIII at their wedding in France, June 1937.

HATRED AT WORK The Nazis organise a boycott of Jewish shops in 1933. The sign reads 'Germans protect yourselves. Don't buy from Jews'.

need for something to believe in – had not diminished. Religion was much discussed in the 1920s and 30s – there were more books on religious subjects in circulation than ever before, and prominent clergymen contributed frequently to popular magazines. Yet, as Allen again put it, 'all this discussion was itself a sign that for millions of people religion had become a debatable subject instead of being accepted without question among the traditions of the community'. He was referring mainly to urban communities. In rural areas of the United States, and especially in the South, there were many who held strong Fundamentalist beliefs.

THE REVIVALISTS

Religion might, for most, have lost its terrors, but people still felt a need for its power to console, and to explain the mysteries of life and death. This need led to the huge success in the 1920s and 30s of revivalist preachers such as Aimee Semple McPherson, with her Temple in Los Angeles, and Gypsy Smith, whose showmanship always attracted crowds in their thousands, produced numerous converts – and also raised vast sums of money.

McPherson reinterpreted the faith in modern terms with songs such as :

'I've been "listening-in" to Heaven,
And I've had a glorious time,
I have heard such wondrous singing,
And the music it was fine.'

Gypsy Smith would address London crowds with the words: 'Not a cent of your money will come to me; so that I can hit you as hard as I like. Some of you say: "How are you paid?" Do not ask rude questions! I am paid by the committee from another source. Hands up those who are glad to see me here! Now put them in your pockets!'

The religious impulse also led to a growth in membership of some of the smaller religious sects such as the Christian Scientists, Jehovah's Witnesses and Seventh Day Adventists. It led to a greatly increased interest in Chinese and Indian religion and philosophy. The Indian mystic, Krishnamurti, had a huge following in Germany and Britain. Major-General Fuller, the British tank warfare expert, became an enthusiast for Yoga; and the poet T.S. Eliot introduced quotations from Buddhist and Hindu scriptures into his poetry. It led numbers of mainly upper-class intellectuals, such as Graham Greene and Evelyn Waugh, to convert to Roman Catholicism. It led to the success of the 'Oxford Group' movement, founded by the

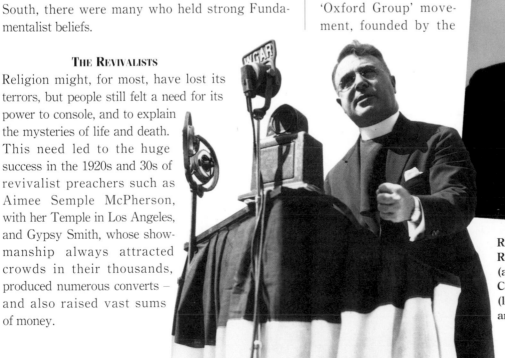

RELIGIOUS PASSIONS Rev Frank Buchman (above) in 1932. Rev Charles Coughlin (left) used radio to arouse hatred.

THE MONKEY TRIAL AND THE RELIGIOUS DIVIDE

IN THE UNITED STATES of the 1920s the religious community was divided broadly into two camps. On the one hand, the Fundamentalists, who believed in the truth of the Bible and rejected any scientific teaching that conflicted with it. On the other, the Modernists or Liberals who were trying to adjust their beliefs to the scientific spirit of the age. The Fundamentalists were especially numerous in the Southern states, and more united and determined in their beliefs than the Modernists. In particular, they wanted to outlaw the teaching of the theory of evolution.

In 1925 the Tennessee legislature, which was dominated by Fundamentalists, passed a bill making it illegal for any teacher in a state-funded school 'to teach any theory that denies the story of the Divine creation of man as taught in the Bible, and to teach instead that man has descended from a lower order of animals'.

In the small town of Dayton, Tennessee, a group of men decided, half in jest, to put the new law to the test by persuading one of their number, a young biology teacher named John Thomas Scopes, to be caught teaching evolution to one of his pupils. Scopes agreed and was duly arrested, and Dayton was catapulted into the national news. The prominent lawyer William Jennings Bryan, a former Secretary of State and presidential candidate, volunteered his services to the prosecution. The equally prominent Clarence Darrow acted for the defence, paid for by the American Civil Liberties Union.

ADVERSARIES Defence lawyer Clarence Seward Darrow (left) and former US Secretary of State William Jennings Bryan (right) in court, 1925.

The trial was conducted in the small courthouse of Dayton in a sweltering July. Simple Tennessee farmers flocked to it with their families to hear about this new-fangled evolution theory, along with revivalist preachers and newspapermen from all over the country. Cable companies conveyed reports of the proceedings, which became known as the 'Monkey Trial' to news agencies in London, which in turn supplied coverage to newspapers as far away as Russia, China and Japan.

The climax came on the afternoon of July 20, when Clarence Darrow put Bryan on the stand as an expert on the Bible, and then questioned him about his Fundamentalist beliefs. Did he, speaking as a lawyer, really believe that Jonah had been swallowed by a whale and survived? Did

he believe Eve was created out of Adam's rib? That the world was created in 4004 BC? Could he explain where Cain had found his wife, when no woman but Eve had yet been created? Hot, angry and flustered (he was to die less than a week later), Bryan affirmed his beliefs before a sceptical and embarrassed audience. The next morning the judge halted the questioning and ordered the previous afternoon's testimony to be removed from the record.

The defence, not permitted to call scientific evidence, decided that their best course was to give up the case at Dayton and go on to an appeal before the Tennessee Supreme Court. Scopes was found guilty and fined $100. The Supreme Court upheld the judgment but freed Scopes on a technicality.

HEAVEN'S ABOVE American evangelist Aimee McPherson, in a state of ecstasy as she addresses an audience in California in 1926.

Adolf Hitler had wooed the churches on his rise to power, and had found support among both Protestant and Catholic clergy. Once the National Socialists had consolidated their position, they set up a National Church sympathetic to their nationalist and racist views. The more extreme among their number, however, were utterly opposed to Christianity, which they regarded as a religion for weaklings, based on Jewish foundations. Serious attempts were made to create a neo-pagan religion based in the Germanic past. At the party rally at Nuremberg in 1934 the Hitler Youth sang:

'No evil priest can prevent us from feeling that we are the children of Hitler. We follow not Christ, but Horst Wessel. Away with incense and holy water. The Church can go hang for all we care. The Swastika brings salvation on Earth. I want to follow it step by step. Baldur von Schirach, take me along!'

American Frank Buchman, which used modern advertising methods to appeal to young clergymen and university undergraduates with its own brand of muscular Christianity. The need to believe led many thousands towards Marxism and membership of the Communist Party (particularly with the onset of the Great Depression); and many others were attracted to the equally absorbing doctrines and passions of the extreme Right.

In the SS, where the neopagan movement was particularly strong, marriages took place in oak-panelled rooms decorated with runic symbols. The bridal pair faced a ritual basin in which an eternal flame was lit to symbolise the fire of the hearth. They then exchanged rings, bread and salt, and the husband gave the wife his SS dagger and received another from his senior officer in exchange. At SS christenings the child was carried on a Teutonic shield. SS Christmas celebrations were held on December 21, and the very expression 'Christmas' was banned in the war years. This neopaganism, like the attempts to coin new, Teutonic names for the months of the year, did not penetrate far beyond the circle of Heinrich Himmler and the fanatics of Aryanism. Although the German churches for the most part maintained a silence on the regime's anti-Semitism, many churchmen openly opposed its other excesses.

SCANDAL!

British newspaper readers in 1932 were titillated by the story of Mr Harold Davidson, vicar of Stiffkey in Norfolk, who was defrocked by the Church of England after allegations of sexual impropriety. Later, the disgraced vicar tried to earn a living by a variety of means, including lion-taming, and was finally mauled to death by a lion.

CRIME AND PUNISHMENT

The 1920s and 30s were remarkably crime-free on the whole,

but in the United States, Prohibition produced irresistible temptations for organised

criminals – and made some of the worst world-famous.

IN THE YEARS just after the end of the First World War there was some public concern in Europe about juvenile delinquency, because of the number of young boys whose fathers had been absent during the war, or had not returned home from it. Juvenile crime did increase slightly. So, too, did traffic offences – but for the simple reason that there were many more motor cars. And there was a steady increase in crimes of larceny, perhaps because more people now insured their possessions and therefore reported them when they were stolen. But despite the high levels of unemployment, the 1920s and 30s in Britain and in Europe generally were surprisingly law-abiding. The restrictive licensing laws introduced in Britain during the war, coupled with the fact that life now offered alternative entertainments to heavy drinking in pubs, partly explained the marked decline in brutish public drunkenness that had been a familiar feature of the poorer parts of towns in the early 1900s. Crime on the streets (apart from prostitution and political violence) was virtually unknown.

NEW YORK'S FINEST
A New York City traffic policeman on duty in Harlem, 1925.

CRIME WAVE **A cops-and-robbers boxed game of the 1930s.**

Criminals rarely used firearms – the most ruthless relied mainly on the razor, the knife and the cosh – and the murder rate was actually lower than before 1914. In Britain, between 1923 and 1939, it was lower than it had been at any time since the 1830s.

Organised crime barely existed. The gang warfare of Glasgow in the 1930s attracted attention mainly because it was so unusual. Most murders, especially in Britain, were domestic ones. The interwar years were in fact something of a Golden Age for the British domestic murder. Feeling otherwise relatively unthreatened in their lives and for their property, the public revelled in the drama and the gory details of the murder trials which were lavishly reported in the popular newspapers of the time. The most lurid novels could scarcely compete with 'The Brides in the Bath' or the 'Brighton Trunk Murders' or the case of the solicitor, Armstrong, who served arsenic at tea time.

CAPONE AND DILLINGER

The situation in the United States was rather different. Its many small towns and affluent residential areas were probably as peaceful and law-abiding as any in the world, but in general it was a more violent and unruly country, with easier access and readier resort to firearms. Much of the violence was associated with American industrial relations. In 1920, Congress introduced Prohibition, which criminalised what had hitherto been the normal and legal practice of producing, selling and consuming alcoholic drinks. The results of this were, almost without exception, disastrous. Many of those who had drunk only moderately before began to drink heavily; many who

DRINK PROBLEM Revellers celebrating the repeal of the unpopular Prohibition (above) in 1933. A large illegal still (right) found by the police in Washington, DC.

had drunk only beer turned to spirits; and many who had never touched alcohol were now drawn to it. The vast amounts of money offered by the illicit trade in liquor enabled the large-scale corruption of policemen, judges and public officials. Its most permanent effect was to stimulate the growth of organised crime under the leadership of criminals such as Al Capone, ruthless in the violent enforcement of their will. In 1931 the *New York World* sceptically summed up the benefits of Prohibition in a poem:

> *Prohibition is an awful flop.*
> *We like it.*
> *It can't stop what it's meant to stop.*
> *We like it.*
> *It's left a trail of graft and slime,*
> *It's filled our land with vice and crime,*
> *It don't prohibit worth a dime,*
> *Nevertheless we're for it.*

After Prohibition was repealed in 1933, the criminal gangs simply turned their attention to the unions, and to gambling, loan sharking, prostitution and protection rackets. The damage had been done. The misery of the Depression in the United States also revived an old type of criminal: the armed bank robber, who now benefited from the automobile to speed his getaway. Criminals such as John Dillinger, 'Pretty Boy' Floyd, 'Baby Face' Nelson, 'Machine Gun' Kelly, 'Ma' Baker, and Bonnie Parker and Clyde Barrow became legends and, given the hatred for banks at that time, attracted considerable public sympathy. One man in Indianapolis wrote of Dillinger, the FBI's Public Enemy Number One: 'Dillinger does not rob poor people. He robs those who became rich by robbing poor people. I am for Johnnie.' A federal commission later reported that public tolerance of violence during the 1930s was the highest in American history. Law-abiding people who had never seen a pistol grew used to talking casually of rods,

CIVIL RIGHTS In 1922 black people paraded in Washington, DC to protest against lynchings. In 1936, at Boyston, Georgia (left), a lynch mob wrest Lint Shaw from officers and hang him. He had been charged with criminal assault and stabbing.

roscoes and equalisers. Even the bootlegging gangsters of the Prohibition era, who turned their violence mainly on each other, were romanticised.

Hollywood fed the public interest in violent crime with 50 gangster films a year, and the fictional career of Dick Tracy, a detective who tended to shoot criminals rather than take them to court, was followed by millions in the comic papers and on children's radio. A man the police claimed to be John Dillinger was gunned down by the FBI in 1934 after leaving a cinema showing a gangster film – although some authorities believe that the real Dillinger fled to the West, and lived on until 1972.

During the interwar years, most Western countries began to place a greater emphasis on the reformative aspects of treating criminals. In Germany, for example, the Reich Criminal Court Law of 1923 tried to establish the principle of educational rehabilitation for young offenders and, in Britain, the Children and Young Persons Act of 1933 put forward probation and borstal training as an alternative to prison for offenders under the age of 21. For adult offenders, too, efforts were made to reduce the number of prison sentences by imposing fines, probation or suspended *(continued on page 148)*

GOOD WOMEN AND TRUE

The first women jurors in Britain were sworn in at Bristol in July 1920, and the prosecuting counsel in the opening case announced that he was the first person ever to use the words 'Ladies and Gentlemen of the Jury' in an English court. Six months later, the first women jurors were sworn in at the Old Bailey in London. Of the 50 women called, nearly half were excused, some of them on seemingly quite trivial grounds. One was released because she felt 'too nervous', another after stating that she thought 'others would enjoy the experience more'.

THE HEYDAY OF THE THRILLER

THE DETECTIVE NOVEL can be traced back to such 19th-century writers as Wilkie Collins and Edgar Allan Poe, but it came into its own in the 1920s and 30s. During this time some of the most famous fictional detectives appeared: Agatha Christie's Hercule Poirot (in the *Mysterious Affair at Styles*, 1920); Dorothy Sayers's Lord Peter Wimsey (in *Whose Body?* 1923); Frederic Dannay and Manfred Lee's Ellery Queen (in *The Roman Hat Mystery*, 1929); Dashiell Hammett's Sam Spade (in *The Maltese Falcon*, 1930) and his Nora and Nick Charles (in *The Thin Man*, 1932).

In the same period the Belgian-born writer Georges Simenon was producing stories by the hundred, and novels by the dozen, far outstripping even the highly prolific British writer Edgar Wallace. The heroes of these novels are seldom police detectives. English writers, in the tradition of Conan Doyle's Sherlock Holmes, favoured the gentleman amateur detective, and the police themselves are often portrayed as

QUEEN OF CRIME Agatha Christie (above) was one of the leading crime writers of the 'body in the library' genre popular in the 1920s-30s. A lurid illustration (above right) from a pulp crime-fiction book of the 1930s.

clumsy plodders, either resentful of, or deferentially grateful for, the hero's brilliant investigative skills.

The classic English detective stories of the period are frequently set in the country village, with its squire, its gossiping neighbours, its vicar and doctor. They are essentially narrative puzzles, often of the 'locked room' type, with red herrings and clues abounding. Agatha Christie is still the unrivalled queen of this type of story.

American writers, in contrast, favoured the private detective as hero, and their settings were the gritty – often sordid – reality of urban life. Dashiell Hammett was the out-

standing writer of the 'hard-boiled' school of pulp novels. As with his great successor, Raymond Chandler, Hammett's hero-detective is tough and cynical, but still humane, the one incorruptible man who stands out in a corrupt world.

THE THIN MAN Dashiell Hammett in 1934. He created a new kind of private detective – the man of principle in a corrupt world.

BEST SELLER Edgar Wallace in New York, 1931. His publisher's slogan was 'It is impossible not to be thrilled by Edgar Wallace'.

PROHIBITION AND GANGSTERS

The lure of huge profits from the illicit liquor trade led to violence and murder on the streets of Chicago.

IN 1920 a Chicago gangster called Johnny Torrio, recognising the fortune that could be made from the now-illicit liquor business, hired a young hoodlum called Alphonse Capone to lead the enforcement side of the operation, scaring off or, if necessary, eliminating rival bootleggers and intimidating speakeasy proprietors into buying his wares.

Capone set himself up in an office and had business cards printed with the legend:

ALPHONSE CAPONE
Second Hand Furniture Dealer

2220 South Wabash Avenue

By 1923 Capone was believed to have 700 men at his disposal, many armed with Thompson sub-machine guns. By 1925 he had complete control of the Chicago suburb of Cicero, even appointing his own mayor, and had established his headquarters at the Hawthorne Hotel. Torrio, meanwhile, had faded into the background; Capone was now the Big Shot.

In 1926 one of Chicago's rival gangs, the O'Banions, drove past the Hawthorne Hotel in eight cars and raked it with machine-gun fire (after carefully scaring away innocent bystanders by firing blanks). Casualties were light, and Capone himself survived unscathed. Seven of the O'Banion gang paid for the action on St Valentine's Day in 1929, when they were herded into a garage and mown down with sub-machine guns by Al Capone's men, who were dressed as police.

In all there were over 500 gang murders in 1930s Chicago, and few of the killers were ever apprehended, let alone convicted. Dion O'Banion, the leader of the O'Banion gang, had been killed earlier. Frederick Allen described how:

'O'Banion was a bootlegger and a gangster by night, but a florist by day: a strange and complex character, a connoisseur of orchids and of manslaughter. One morning a sedan drew up outside his flower shop and three men got out, leaving the fourth at the wheel. The three men had apparently taken good care to win O'Banion's trust, for although he always carried three guns, now for the moment he was off his guard as he advanced among the flowers to meet his visitors. The middle man of the three cordially shook hands with O'Banion – *and then held on* – while

RETRIBUTION Members of the O'Banion gang lie dead on the floor of a Chicago garage after the St Valentine's Day massacre, 1929.

GET·DILLINGER!
$15,000 Reward
A PROCLAMATION

WHEREAS, One John Dillinger stands charged officially with numerous felonies including murder in several states and his banditry and depredation stamp him as an outlaw, a fugitive from justice and a vicious menace to life and property:

NOW, THEREFORE, We, Paul McNutt, Governor of Indiana; George White, Governor of Ohio; F. B. Olson, Governor of Minnesota; William A. Comstock, Governor of Michigan; and Henry Horner, Governor of Illinois, do hereby proclaim and offer a reward of Five Thousand Dollars ($5,000.00) to be paid to the person or persons who apprehend and deliver the said John Dillinger into the custody of any sheriff of any of the above-mentioned states or his duly authorized agent.

THIS IS IN ADDITION TO THE $10,000.00 OFFERED BY THE FEDERAL GOVERNMENT FOR THE ARREST OF JOHN DILLINGER.

HERE IS HIS FINGERPRINT CLASSIFICATION and DESCRIPTION. — FILE THIS FOR IDENTIFICATION PURPOSES.

PUBLIC ENEMY John Dillinger, wanted for murder and other felonies in several states. To escape conviction he altered his fingerprints with acid.

his two companions put six bullets into the gangster-florist. The three conspirators walked out, climbed into the sedan, and departed. They were never brought to justice, and it is not recorded that any of them hung themselves to trees in remorse. O'Banion had a first-class funeral, gangster style: a ten-thousand dollar casket, twenty-six truck-loads of flowers, and among them a basket of flowers which bore the touching inscription, "From Al".'

Capone's business was mainly based on beer-running. In 1927, federal agents estimated that he controlled liquor revenues worth $60 million annually

TAX EVADER Al Capone was finally convicted on tax evasion charges in 1931.

– Chicago alone had 10 000 speakeasies. That same year, he spent some $260 000 financing the re-election campaign of the city's mayor 'Big Bill' Thompson. His annual outgoings to the politicians, judges and policemen on his payroll probably added up to more than $30 million. He also liked to give generously to good causes, ranging from restoration funds for churches to soup kitchens for the poor during the Depression.

His personal fortune, meanwhile, was estimated to be at least $20 million. He rode around Chicago in an armoured car. When he went to the theatre, he was attended by a bodyguard of 18 men in dinner jackets. He entertained guests at his estate in Florida and from his Chicago office he called politicians with his daily orders. Nothing, it seemed, could touch him. When he was finally imprisoned in 1931, it was on charges of federal tax evasion. He was then 32 years old.

Capone spent 11 years in prison – many of them at Alcatraz. On release in 1939, broken by the experience and degenerating physically and mentally due to syphilis, he retired to his home on Palm Island, Florida. He died in 1947.

Prohibition was finally repealed in 1933. Deprived of its rich profits, criminals turned to bank robbery and other activities, especially gambling, vice, extortion,

BONNIE AND CLYDE The famous crime duo Bonnie Parker and Clyde Barrow, 1932.

loan-sharking and union racketeering. Bank robbers such as John Dillinger, 'Machine Gun' Kelly, Bonnie Parker and Clyde Barrow were fought by J. Edgar Hoover, the head of the FBI, and his G-men. Meanwhile, the Mafia organised crime on a larger, more profitable and efficient scale. But Hoover steadfastly refused to acknowledge the existence of the Mafia.

DEADLY FRIENDS George 'Machine Gun' Kelly and his wife, Kathryn.

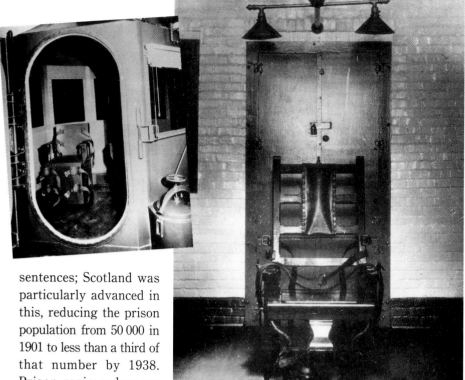

sentences; Scotland was particularly advanced in this, reducing the prison population from 50 000 in 1901 to less than a third of that number by 1938. Prison regimes became less severe – prisoners no longer had their hair cropped, and the 'silent system' in which prisoners

DEAD ENDS The electric chair at Trenton, New Jersey (above). A gas chamber, San Quentin, California (left). Both are forms of execution used in the United States.

could neither speak nor be spoken to was largely abolished. In the 1930s, there were experiments with 'open' prisons, in which prisoners were allowed freedom of movement within the prison grounds.

But society's views about the proper treatment of criminals were still uneasily balanced between theories of reform, deterrence and retribution. The regime in most prisons was still far from 'soft'. Solitary confinement was still widely used for offences within the prison. The work given to prisoners as an alternative to punishment might well be nothing more redemptive than sewing mailbags, and the sentence of 'hard labour', whether stonebreaking at Dartmoor or labouring in the chain-gangs of the American South, was still used. From time to time there were prison riots, such as the one which broke out at Dartmoor in 1932, and which was sparked off by the poor food prisoners were expected to eat and rumours of assaults on prisoners by the warders.

THE RATTENBURY CASE

THE BRITISH WRITER James Agate covered the trial of Mrs Rattenbury and Stoner, her young lover and chauffeur, for the *Daily Express* in 1935. Stoner was found guilty and condemned to death. Mrs Rattenbury was acquitted, but six days later committed suicide by first stabbing herself and then drowning.

❛ The facts were very simple and hardly disputed. Mrs Rattenbury, aged 38, had been the mistress of her 18-year-old chauffeur named Stoner. Somebody had hit her husband over the head with a mallet, both of them having at one time or another taken the blame on themselves.

It was very like the three French major novelists. The way in which the woman debauched the boy so that he slept with her every night with her six-year-old son in the room, and the husband who had his own bedroom remaining cynically indifferent – this was pure Balzac. In the box Mrs Rattenbury looked and talked exactly as I have always imagined Emma Bovary looked and

talked. Pure Flaubert. At last there was that part of her evidence in which she described how, trying to bring her husband round, she first accidentally trod on his false teeth and then tried to put them back in his mouth so that he could speak to her. That was pure Zola . . . Counsel asked Mrs Rattenbury what her first thought had been when her lover . . . told her what he had done. She replied, "to protect him." This is the kind of thing which Balzac would have called sublime. ❜

HARD LABOUR Convicts (wearing their prison uniforms) working in a quarry in Georgia, *c.*1920.

Britain still sentenced young offenders to strokes with the birch, but resorting to corporal punishment became less common. In 1938 there were 17 floggings for robbery with violence and 43 juveniles were birched for various offences, compared with over 3000 floggings and birchings in 1900. Corporal punishment was rare elsewhere in the developed world.

As the ultimate sanction Britain, the United States and most of the countries of Europe still imposed the death penalty. Indeed, it was mandatory for murder in most countries, although increasingly judges and juries found grounds for commuting the sentence to one of life imprisonment. In Britain by the 1930s almost half of all murderers convicted had their sentences commuted on grounds of 'insanity' or 'unfitness to plead'. Where the death penalty was imposed, hanging was the favoured method in Britain and the Commonwealth, beheading in France and Germany. In the United States, where the method varied from state to state, there were still about 150 executions each year in the early 1930s, but the number began to fall sharply towards the end of the interwar years. In Germany many of the most violent instincts of society were channelled into militant political activity in the street gangs of the extreme Left and Right. From 1933 the National Socialists gained much public approval as a 'law and order' government. Under their rule, there was a sharp drop in most kinds of serious crime.

THE FASCINATION OF CRIME

People in the interwar years seemed fascinated by crime. They crowded to watch gangster movies in the cinema, read thrillers and detective novels and avidly followed the accounts of murders in the newspapers, which did not hesitate to give the most detailed accounts. In this respect they were not much different from their Victorian predecessors, who had revelled in the accounts of dastardly crimes covered by periodicals such as *The Police Gazette*. But such periodicals had sold mainly to the lower classes, whereas now an interest in crime stories seemed to be enjoyed by everyone. Perhaps the excitements of the life of crime could be enjoyed vicariously because real life for most people was, most of the time and in most places, safe, crime-free and perhaps a little dull. Or perhaps reading about crime, and watching it at the cinema, offered a distraction from the threat of more terrifying dangers in the real world that, as the 1930s came towards its end, loomed larger in people's lives.

TIME CHART

WORLD EVENTS

CELEBRATION Armistice Day, Washington DC, November 11, 1918.

1918 The Treaty of Brest-Litovsk ends war between Russia and Germany.

Tsar Nicholas and his family are murdered by the Bolsheviks.

The German Kaiser Wilhelm II abdicates and a German Republic is proclaimed.

An armistice is signed at Compiegne, bringing World War I to an end.

1919 The left-wing 'Spartacus' uprising in Germany is suppressed.

The Versailles Peace Treaty is signed.

The German fleet is scuttled at Scapa Flow, off Scotland.

1920 The attempted 'Kapp' Putsch by monarchists in Germany collapses after a General Strike.

The League of Nations Assembly meets for the first time.

Warren G. Harding becomes US President.

1921 German war reparations are set at 269 billion gold marks.

The Irish Free State is established, with a separate parliament in Dublin.

Mahatma Gandhi emerges as a leader in India's struggle for independence.

PRESIDENT Warren G. Harding in 1920.

ARTS AND LEISURE

1919 Jack Dempsey defeats fellow American Jess Willard for the world heavyweight boxing championship.

Walter Gropius founds the Bauhaus in Weimar.

1920 Paul Whiteman's jazz band visits Europe.

The first exhibition of Dada art is held in Cologne.

1921 Baseball superstar Babe Ruth scores 177 runs in a season, an all-time record.

BASEBALL LEGEND Babe Ruth in 1923.

WORKING-CLASS WRITER Novelist D.H. Lawrence, c.1925.

BOOKS: Lytton Strachey *Eminent Victorians* (1918); Wilfred Owen's *Poems* (published posthumously in 1920); D.H. Lawrence *Women in Love* (1921).

FILMS: Charlie Chaplin *Shoulder Arms* (1918) and *The Kid* (1920); Robert Weine's expressionist masterpiece *The Cabinet of Doctor Caligari* (1919); Robert Flaherty's ground-breaking documentary *Nanook of the North* (1920).

THEATRE AND MUSIC: Bela Bartok *Bluebeard's Castle* (1918); Bernard Shaw *Heartbreak House* (1919); Sergei Prokofiev *The Love of Three Oranges* (1921).

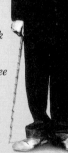

THE TRAMP Charlie Chaplin.

CHANGING SOCIETY

AVIATORS J.W. Alcock (left) and A. Brown after their record flight.

1918 In Britain an Education Act raises the school-leaving age to 14.

Women over 30 are given the vote.

1919 Alcock and Brown make the first transatlantic flight in 16 hrs 27 mins.

In Germany, women over 20 get the vote for the first time.

In Britain Lady Astor becomes the first woman MP to take a seat in Parliament.

1920 The Radio Corporation of America is formed.

Prohibition begins in the United States.

American women are given the vote for the first time.

1921 Marie Stopes establishes the first birth-control clinic in London.

Capital punishment is abolished in Sweden.

PROHIBITION Federal agents pour whiskey into a sewer.

1 9 2 2 – 1 9 2 5

1922 In India, Mahatma Gandhi is imprisoned for civil disobedience.

Germany and the Soviet Union sign the Rapallo Treaty restoring diplomatic and trade relations.

Mussolini establishes a Fascist government in Italy.

Mustafa Kemal proclaims a Turkish Republic.

1923 The Union of

Mahatma Gandhi, 1869-1948.

Soviet Socialist Republics is established.

France occupies the Ruhr as a response to Germany's failure to pay reparations.

Lloyd George's wartime coalition government falls and Stanley Baldwin replaces Bonar Law as Britain's Conservative Prime Minister.

Due to hyperinflation, the German mark becomes virtually worthless.

Hitler's attempted 'beer-hall' *Putsch* in Munich fails, and he is arrested and imprisoned.

The *Rentenmark* is introduced to restore the German currency.

1924 Lenin dies.

Ramsay MacDonald becomes Prime Minister in Britain's first Labour government.

Greece proclaims a republic after deposing King George II.

In Britain, the Conservatives defeat Labour in the General Election.

The Republican Calvin Coolidge is elected US President.

1925 Released from prison, Hitler resumes leadership of the National Socialist Party.

In Germany, Hindenburg is elected Reich President.

Britain returns to the Gold Standard.

Ramsay MacDonald was Labour's first Prime Minister.

1922 Howard Carter discovers Tutankhamun's Tomb in Egypt and reveals its treasures to an astonished world.

1923 English cricketer Jack Hobbs scores his 100th first-class century.

French tennis player Suzanne Lenglen wins the women's singles at Wimbledon for the fifth time.

1924 In the Olympics the Scottish runner Eric Liddell refuses to take part in the qualifying heat of the 100 metres relay because it is held on a Sunday, but goes on to set a new record for the 400 metres.

Puccini dies. His last opera, *Turandot*, is performed.

1925 The Bauhaus moves to Walter Gropius's new buildings at Dessau in Germany.

Paris hosts a great exhibition of Decorative Arts, which creates a new

style, known as Art Deco, in fashions, architecture and furniture.

Josephine Baker creates a sensation in Paris, starring in the *Revue Negre*.

NIGHTLIFE **Josephine Baker in revue costume in the mid 1920s.**

BOOKS: James Joyce's *Ulysses* (1922) is banned almost everywhere; Sinclair Lewis *Babbit* (1922); T.S. Eliot *The Waste Land* (1922); Aldous Huxley *Antic Hay* (1923); E.M. Forster *A Passage to India* (1924); Thomas Mann *The Magic Mountain*, F. Scott Fitzgerald *The Great Gatsby*, Franz Kafka *The Trial*, Anita Loos *Gentlemen Prefer Blondes*, P.G. Wodehouse *Carry on, Jeeves*, all published in 1925, in their different ways sum up the spirit of the 1920s.

FILMS: Fritz Lang *Dr Mabuse* (1922); Sergei Eisenstein *The Battleship Potemkin* (1923); Cecil B. De Mille *The Ten Commandments* (1924); Douglas Fairbanks stars in *The Thief of Baghdad* (1924); Charlie Chaplin *The Gold Rush* (1925).

THEATRE AND MUSIC: G.B. Shaw *Saint Joan* (1923); George Gershwin *Lady be Good* and *Rhapsody in Blue*; Noel Coward's *The Vortex* and his first successful comedy *Hay Fever* (1925).

1922 The first *Reader's Digest* is published in the United States.

The British Broadcasting Company is formed. (It will become the British Broadcasting Corporation in 1927.)

1923 British law allows women to divorce their husbands for adultery.

Tetanus and diphtheria immunisation introduced.

THE READER'S DIGEST

FEBRUARY 1922

First *Reader's Digest* magazine.

The Duke of York, later George VI, marries Elizabeth Bowes-Lyon.

New York opens the first birth-control clinic.

There are now eight women MPs in Britain.

1924 Imperial Airways, Britain's first national airline, is formed.

The Duke of York and Lady Elizabeth Bowes-Lyon.

The United States grants full citizenship to American Indians.

1925 The first woman governor of a US state elected by Wyoming.

The first in-flight movie is shown on an Imperial Airways Channel crossing.

Tennessee bans the teaching of evolution in state schools on religious grounds.

151

1926 – 1929

WORLD EVENTS

1926 Reza Khan becomes Shah of Persia.

The General Strike in Britain, which grew out of a miners' strike, lasts nine days, but the miners struggle on for six months.

Germany is admitted to the League of Nations.

1927 Allied military control of Germany ends and the troops begin to withdraw from the Rhineland.

There is a General Strike and Socialist riots in Vienna.

DICTATOR Soviet leader, Joseph Stalin, 1879-1953.

1928 There is an all-time record for trading on the New York Stock Exchange.

Fifteen nations sign the Kellog-Briand anti-war pact.

In the USSR, Stalin introduces the first five-year economic plan.

Chiang Kai-shek becomes president of China

The Republican politician Herbert Hoover becomes US President.

Hirohito is enthroned as Emperor of Japan.

1929 Leon Trotsky is expelled from the USSR.

Ramsay MacDonald forms a new Labour government in Britain.

The Wall Street Crash leads to world-wide economic and financial crisis and the Depression.

GENERALISSIMO Nationalist leader Chiang Kai-shek, 1888-1975.

ARTS AND LEISURE

1926 Silent movie star Rudolf Valentino dies, and is mourned by a generation of women.

Greta Garbo makes her American debut, but her greatest films will be made in the 1930s.

1927 Al Jolson stars in *The Jazz Singer*, the first 'talkie'.

1928 Walt Disney makes the first sound cartoon film, *Steamboat Willie*, starring Mickey Mouse.

At the height of their success, Laurel and Hardy make four films in 1928.

1929 Cartoon characters Popeye and Tintin make their first appearance.

BOOKS: A.A. Milne *Winnie-the-Pooh* (1926); Virginia Woolf *To the Lighthouse* (1927); Evelyn Waugh's first novel *Decline and Fall* (1928); D.H. Lawrence *Lady Chatterley's Lover* (1928). Ernest Hemingway's *A Farewell to Arms* and Robert Graves's *Goodbye to All That*,

both published in 1929, betoken a revived interest in World War I, as does Erich Maria Remarque's novel *All Quiet on the Western Front,* which becomes an international bestseller.

FILMS: Fritz Lang's futuristic fantasy *Metropolis* (1926); Buster Keaton *The General* (1927).

NOVELIST Evelyn Waugh, 1903-66.

THEATRE AND MUSIC: Ziegfeld's musical *Show Boat* with music by Jerome Kern (1927); Gershwin *An American in Paris* (1928); *The Threepenny Opera*, with words by Brecht and music by Kurt Weill, is performed in Berlin (1928); R.C. Sheriff's *Journey's End* (1929) revives memories of the war

and is a huge success; *Toad of Toad Hall*, A.A. Milne's stage adaptation of Kenneth Grahame's *The Wind in the Willows*, begins its long run as an annual children's play.

ANIMATION Mr and Mrs Walt Disney sleigh-ride with Mickey.

CHANGING SOCIETY

1926 John Logie Baird demonstrates television in London.

Alan Cobham makes a record round-the-world flight in 58 days.

1927 Henry Seagrave sets a land-speed record of over 200 mph.

SPEED RECORD Seagrave speeds along Daytona Beach, Florida.

Charles Lindbergh makes the first solo transatlantic flight.

In the United States, the anarchists Sacco and Vanzetti are executed for murder after a long campaign protesting their innocence.

Pan Am launches the first international flight.

1928 In Britain, over-65s receive their first state pensions.

AVIATRIX Amelia Earhart, 1898-1937.

British women get the vote at 21 (the so-called Flapper Vote).

Amelia Earhart is the first woman to fly the Atlantic. In 1932 she will fly it solo.

Alexander Fleming reports the discovery of penicillin.

The *Graf Zeppelin* makes the first commercial transatlantic flight.

1929 In Chicago seven members of the O'Banion gang are gunned down in what becomes known throughout the world as the St Valentine's Day massacre.

1 9 3 0 – 1 9 3 3

THIRD REICH Hindenburg and Hitler, 1933.

1930 Stalin collectivises agriculture in the USSR.

The Nazi Party win 100 seats from moderates in German elections.

1931 The Nazis demand Germany's withdrawal from the League of Nations.

The collapse of Austria's main bank leads to a banking crisis.

Ramsay MacDonald forms a coalition National government in Britain

Japan invades Manchuria.

The British Dominions become fully self-governing.

1932 The Japanese proclaim the Manchukuo Republic in Manchuria and invade Shanghai.

Field-Marshal Hindenburg re-elected German president.

After Reichstag elections the Nazis become the largest party.

The Democrat Franklin Roosevelt is elected US President.

1933 Adolf Hitler becomes German Chancellor.

NEW DEAL The 1932 Roosevelt campaign.

The German Reichstag building is burnt to the ground.

The Nazis begin mass arrests of opponents and open the first concentration camp at Dachau. An Enabling Law provides Adolf Hitler with absolute power.

President Roosevelt closes US banks for four days to avert total collapse and sets up the NRA (National Recovery Administration).

WORLD EVENTS

1930 The Australian cricketer Don Bradman makes a record Test match score of 334 against England.

The American golfer Bobby Jones wins the British Amateur Championship and the British Open.

Marlene Dietrich leaps to stardom in Josef von Sternberg's *The Blue Angel*.

1931 Malcolm Campbell sets a world

RECORD-BREAKER Malcolm Campbell in *Bluebird*.

land-speed record of 246.09 mph in his car *Bluebird* at Daytona Beach, Florida. Constantly breaking his own records, he will eventually take the record to over 300 mph.

1932 American sculptor Alexander Calder exhibits the first mobiles in Paris.

1933 'Bodyline' bowling makes the MCC's Test tour of Australia controversial.

BOOKS: W.H. Auden *Poems* (1930); Evelyn Waugh *Vile Bodies* (1930); William Faulkner *Sanctuary* (1931); Aldous Huxley *Brave New World* (1932); George Orwell *Down and Out in Paris and London* (1933)

FILMS: Lewis Milestone *All Quiet on the Western Front* (1930); Charlie Chaplin *City Lights* (1931); Garbo stars in *Queen Christina*, and Fay Ray and a large ape star in *King Kong* (1933).

THEATRE AND MUSIC: Noël Coward *Private Lives* (1930) and *Cavalcade* (1931)

STAGE AND SCREEN Lew Ayres (above), star of *All Quiet on the Western Front*. Noël Coward (left) leaves for Canada, 1934.

ARTS AND LEISURE

1930 Amy Johnson is the first woman to fly from Britain to Australia.

There are more than 4.5 million unemployed in the United States; more than 3 million in Germany; more than 2 million in Britain.

The Empire State Building is opened in New York, for many years the world's tallest building.

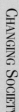

SKYSCRAPER The Empire State Building was the tallest in the world at 1250 ft (381m) high.

Unemployment in the United States is more than 8 million; in Germany more than 5 million; in Britain 2.75 million.

1932 Amelia Earhart is the first woman to fly the Atlantic solo.

There are violent clashes between police and demonstrators in London after a hunger march.

George V makes the first royal Christmas Broadcast. There are now 3 million wireless licences in Britain, where unemployment reaches its peak of 3.75 million.

ENGINEERING Sydney Harbour Bridge under construction, 1931.

1933 Wily Post completes the first solo round-the-world flight.

In the United States the much-ignored Prohibition is repealed.

CHANGING SOCIETY

1934 – 1936

WORLD EVENTS

1934 Oswald Mosley urges a Fascist dictatorship in Britain.

Hitler and Mussolini meet in Venice.

In the 'Night of the Long Knives' Hitler arrests and executes the leaders of the SA, the Nazis' brown-shirted private army, and other political opponents.

Austrian Chancellor Dollfuss is assassinated by Austrian Nazis in Vienna.

Hindenburg dies, and Hitler becomes sole and supreme ruler of Germany.

In the USSR Stalin is purging the Communist Party. There may be up to 10 million people in labour camps.

The Conservative Stanley Baldwin succeeds Ramsay MacDonald as British Prime Minister.

ABDICATION Edward VIII broadcasts his abdication, 1936.

In China the Red Army begins its legendary 'Long March' after breaking out of a Nationalist blockade. It will march 6000 miles, and will be fighting most of the way.

Italy invades Ethiopia.

1936 King George V dies and is succeeded by Edward VIII.

German troops march into the demilitarised Rhineland.

Civil War breaks out in Spain after an army revolt against the Republican government.

At the 11th Olympic Games in Berlin the black American athlete Jesse Owens challenges Nazi notions of Aryan supremacy by winning four gold medals.

Mussolini proclaims the Rome-Berlin Axis.

After 11 months the uncrowned Edward VIII abdicates 'to be with the woman I love', Mrs Wallis Simpson. He is succeeded by his brother, now George VI.

ARTS AND LEISURE

1934 Louis Armstrong, Cab Calloway and Coleman Hawkins appear in London.

1935 *Becky Sharp* is the first full-colour talking movie.

Mary Pickford divorces Douglas Fairbanks.

Allen Lane launches Penguin Books in Britain.

Malcolm Campbell sets a new land-speed record of 301 mph.

T.E. Lawrence, 'Lawrence of Arabia',

PAPERBACK The first Penguin, price sixpence.

GONE WITH THE WIND Clark Gable reads the book of the movie.

author of *The Seven Pillars of Wisdom*, dies in a motorcycle accident.

1936 Joe DiMaggio plays his first World Series for the New York Yankees.

BOOKS: Scott Fitzgerald *Tender is the Night* (1934); Evelyn Waugh *A Handful of Dust* (1934); Christopher Isherwood *Mr Norris Changes Trains* (1935). Margaret Mitchell's *Gone With the Wind* (1936) is a runaway bestseller.

FILMS: *It Happened One Night*, star-

ring Clark Gable and Claudette Colbert (1934); Alfred Hitchcock *The Thirty-Nine Steps* (1935); Chaplin's *Modern Times* (1936); Alexander Korda's futurist fantasy *Things to Come* (1936); Leni Riefenstahl's documentary of the Nazis' Nuremberg Rally, *The Triumph of the Will* (1936); Greta Garbo in *Camille* (1936).

THEATRE AND MUSIC: George Gershwin *Porgy and Bess* (1935); Prokofiev *Peter and the Wolf* (1936).

ROMANTIC COMEDY Claudette Colbert and Clark Gable in the film *It Happened One Night*.

CHANGING SOCIETY

1934 Driving tests become compulsory in Britain.

Wimbledon permits women players to wear shorts for the first time.

Bonnie and Clyde are killed by police in an ambush in Louisiana.

1935 A 30 mph speed limit in built-up areas is introduced in Britain.

Union membership becomes lawful in the United States.

In Germany the Nazis legalise anti-Semitism in the Nuremberg Laws.

Roosevelt introduces a Social Security

AIRSHIP The airship *Hindenburg* in flight, 1936.

Act in the United States, providing pensions, unemployment and sickness

benefits, and help for the disabled.

In Germany non-belief in Nazism becomes legal grounds for divorce.

Pan Am starts a regular trans-Pacific mail and passenger service.

1936 The airship *Hindenburg* crosses the Atlantic in 46 hours.

The Jarrow Hunger Marchers arrive in London.

Crystal Palace is destroyed by fire.

The BBC begins the first high-definition television service from Alexandra Palace in London.

World Events

1937 The Spanish town of Guernica is destroyed by German bombers.

Neville Chamberlain becomes British Prime Minister.

Japanese forces take Peking.

Italy leaves the League of Nations.

1938 Austria and Germany united.

Neville Chamberlain, desperate to avoid war, makes a compromise agreement with Hitler at talks in Munich, and announces 'peace for our time'.

Kristallnacht in Germany. There is widespread destruction of Jewish property and mob violence against Jews.

Germany occupies the Sudeten part of Czechoslovakia.

1939 Germany invades Bohemia and

FASCISMO **The Italian dicator Benito Mussolini, 1883-1945.**

Moravia and occupies Prague.

Italy invades Albania.

APPEASEMENT **Neville Chamberlain, after meeting Hitler, 1938.**

The Spanish Civil War ends.

Hitler and Mussolini sign the 'pact of steel'.

Germany and the USSR sign a non-aggression pact.

Germany invades Poland and World War II begins.

Arts and Leisure

1937 An International Surrealist Exhibition is held in London.

George Gershwin dies.

1938 Picasso's painting *Guernica* is exhibited in London.

English cricketer Len Hutton scores a record 364 runs against Australia.

CROONER **Frank Sinatra made his first record in 1939.**

Helen Wills Moody wins the women's title at Wimbledon for the eighth time.

1939 Frank Sinatra makes his first record, 'All or Nothing at All'. It sells 8000 copies.

WIZARD OF OZ **Judy Garland and the Tin Man.**

BOOKS: John Steinbeck *Of Mice and Men* (1937); Graham Greene *Brighton Rock* (1938); Thornton Wilder *Our Town* (1938); Christopher Isherwood *Goodbye to Berlin* (1939); James Joyce *Finnegan's Wake* (1939); John Steinbeck *The Grapes of Wrath* (1939).

FILMS: Jean Renoir *La Grande Illusion* (1937); Hitchcock *The Lady Vanishes* (1938); William Wyler *Wuthering Heights* (1939); Walt Disney's first full-length cartoon feature film *Snow White and the Seven Dwarfs* (1938); Sergei Eisenstein *Alexander Nevsky* (1939); John Ford *Stagecoach*, starring John Wayne (1939); the young Judy Garland triumphs in *The Wizard of Oz* (1939); David O. Selznick's *Gone With the Wind*, starring Clark Gable and Vivien Leigh, wins nine Oscars (1939).

ULYSSES **James Joyce, the author.**

Changing Society

1937 The airship *Hindenburg* explodes while landing in New Jersey.

George VI is crowned at Westminster Abbey, watched by 50 000 television viewers in the south-east of England.

Amelia Earhart disappears in the course of a flight over the Pacific.

The Nazis open Buchenwald concentration camp.

1938 The first nylon product – toothbrush bristles – appears.

CORONATION **King George VI is crowned at Westminster with due ceremony.**

An Empire flying boat opens the first through service to Australia.

The liner *Queen Elizabeth* is launched.

Gas masks are issued in Britain.

1939 Britain announces first-ever peacetime conscription measures. The call up is limited to men aged 20 and 21.

King George VI visits the New York World Fair.

In Britain the evacuation of children from the cities begins.

In Poland the Nazis begin to round up and deport Jews.

INDEX

ACKNOWLEDGMENTS

ABBREVIATIONS T = Top;
M = Middle; B = Bottom;
R = Right; L = Left.

M.E.P.L. = Mary Evans Picture
Library.
T.B.A. = Toucan Books Archive

1 M.E.P.L. 2-3 Range/Bettmann.
4 Robert Opie Collection, TL;
Range/Bettmann, TR. 5 Victoria &
Albert Museum, London, TL; Kodak
Girl/Science Museum, TR; M.E.P.L.,
ML, MR; Range/Bettmann, BL. 6
Ullstein Bilderdienst. 7 The Royal
Photographic Society. 8 Hulton-
Deutsch, BL. 9 Range/Bettmann;
M.E.P.L., BR. 11 Ullstein
Bilderdienst, TL; Arthur Lockwood,
TR, B. 12 Poster for British Empire
Exhibition, 1925, T.B.A. 13
Copyright © J-P Kernot/*Evening
Meal*, photograph by Bill Brandt. 14
Range/Bettmann. 15 Phot. A.Kertész
© Ministére de la Culture-France.
16 Brown Brothers, BL; Range/
Bettmann/UPI/Library of Congress.
17 Range/Bettmann. 18 Range/
Bettmann, ML; Culver Pictures Inc.,
T. 19 Range/Bettmann, T;
Range/UPI, B. 20 University College,
London, T; John Frost Newspapers,
B. 21 Range/Bettmann, T; Range/
Bettmann/UPI, ML. 22 Range/
Bettmann, BL; Ullstein Bilderdienst,
BR. 23 Range/Bettmann, TR;
M.E.P.L., MR. 24 Batsford Files. 25
Vintage Magazines Co. 26-27
Illustration by Peter Morter. 28
Ullstein Bilderdienst. 29
Range/Bettmann, TL; Hulton-
Deutsch, TR. 30 John Frost
Newspapers, ML; M.E.P.L., TR. 31
Range/Bettmann, T; Copyright © J-P
Kernot/*Northumbrian Miner at his
Evening Meal*, photograph by Bill
Brandt, BL. 32 Library of Congress.
33 Range/Bettmann, TL; Robert Opie
Collection, TR. 34 Range/Bettmann,
BL; Robert Opie Collection, BR. 35
Ullstein Bilderdienst, TR, MR. 36
Range/Bettmann, T, B. 37 Copyright
© J-P Kernot/*Child and Nanny*,
photograph by Bill Brandt, TR;
Robert Opie Collection, MR. 38
T.B.A., T; Photograph by Margaret
Burke-White B. 39 Denver Public
Library, T; Science Museum, BR. 40
Robert Opie Collection. 41 Topham
Picture Source. 42 Robert Opie
Collection, ML; *Illustrated London
News*, B. 43 Hulton-Deutsch, T;
Robert Opie Collection, B. 44 Library
of Congress. 45 Bauhaus Archives,
TR; Ullstein Bilderdienst, B. 46
M.E.P.L., T; Lee Miller Archives, B.
47 Culver Pictures Inc., T; T.B.A., B.
48 T.B.A., T, B. 49 Jerome Darblay,
TR; Batsford Files, ML. 50
Smithsonian Institute, T. Ullstein
Bilderdienst, BL. 51 M.E.P.L., TL,
TR. 52 T.B.A. 53 Ullstein

Bilderdienst, T; T.B.A., B. 54 Library
of Congress, TL; Gordon Russell, TR;
Ullstein Bilderdienst. 55 Edimedie. 56
Hulton-Deutsch, TR, BL, BR. 57
Batsford Files, TL; Philippe Garner,
TR. 58 M.E.P.L., TL, TR; Ullstein
Bilderdienst, BL. 59 Punch
Publications/T.B.A., TR. Popperfoto,
BL. 60 Robert Opie Collection, TL,
TM, TR; Library of Congress, BR. 61
M.E.P.L., TL; Roger-Viollet, TR;
Ullstein Bilderdienst, B. 62 Robert
Opie Collection, TL; Library of
Congress, TR; M.E.P.L., BR. 63
Vintage Magazine Co./© Vogue. 64
M.E.P.L., TL; Ullstein Bilderdienst,
TR. 65 M.E.P.L., T; Ullstein
Bilderdienst, B. 66 T.B.A., TL;
Ullstein Bilderdienst, BL; National
Archives, BR. 67 M.E.P.L., TL;
Ullstein Bilderdienst, TR. 68
Range/Bettmann. 69 Empire
Marketing Board/T.B.A., TL; Robert
Opie Collection, BL; Ullstein
Bilderdienst, BR. 70 M.E.P.L., B. 71
Patrimoine Photographie/Photograph
by Andre Kertész, TL; Robert Opie
Collection, MR; J Lyons & Co. Ltd,
BL. 72, 73, 74 M.E.P.L. 75 Range/
Bettmann. 77 M.E.P.L., T, MR;
Robert Opie Collection, B. 78
M.E.P.L., TR; Range/Bettmann, ML.
79 Smithsonian Institute, T; M.E.P.L.,
B. 80 M.E.P.L., BL; Range/Bettmann,
BR. 81 Range/Bettmann, T; M.E.P.L.,
B. 82 Hulton-Deutsch. 83 Range/
Bettmann, T; Topham Picture
Source, B. 84 Range/Bettmann. 85
M.E.P.L., T; Range/Bettmann, MR.
86 *Buy Canadian Hams and Bacon,
Buy South African Oranges*, posters
by F.C. Herrick, Empire Marketing
Board, TL; Australian Wheat,
poster by A.M. Webb, Empire
Marketing Board, MM. 87 Range/
Bettmann. 89 Barnaby's Picture
Library, TR; Range/Bettmann, BR.
90 UPI/Associated Press. 91 Range/
Bettmann, TL, BR. 92 The Mansell
Collection. 93 Range/Bettmann. 94
Ullstein Bilderdienst. 95 Hulton-
Deutsch, T, B. 96 Barnaby's Picture
Library. 97 Ullstein Bilderdienst, TL;
E.T. Archive, TR. 98-99 Illustration
by Peter Morter. 100 Robert Opie
Collection, T; T.B.A., B. 101 Science
Museum, TL, TR, BR; Robert Opie
Collection, MR. 102 Hulton-Deutsch.
103 Robert Opie Collection, T;
M.E.P.L., BL. 104 T.B.A., TL; Ullstein
Bilderdienst, BR. 105 Ullstein
Bilderdienst, T; M.E.P.L., MR, B. 106
M.E.P.L., T, BR; David Ellery/Queen
Mary Archive, BL. 107 Robert Opie
Collection, TL; M.E.P.L., B. 108
Hulton-Deutsch, TL; Robert Opie
Collection, TR; Ullstein Bilderdienst,
BL. 109 Robert Opie Collection. 110
Science Museum/T.B.A., T; Hulton-
Deutsch, BL. 111 Range/Bettmann/
UPI, T; Robert Opie Collection, MR;
Library of Congress, BR. 112 Hulton-
Deutsch, T; T.B.A., B. 113 M.E.P.L.,
TR; Ullstein Bilderdienst, BL;
M.E.P.L., BR. 114 M.E.P.L., T, BR;

Robert Opie Collection, BL. 115
M.E.P.L., TR; Range/Bettmann, BL;
Hulton-Deutsch, BR. 116 Robert Opie
Collection TL, MR; M.E.P.L., TR; Sir
Francis Dashwood, B. 117 Ullstein
Bilderdienst, TR, BR; M.E.P.L., MM.
118 Range/Bettmann, TL, BR; Robert
Opie Collection, TR. 119 National
Film Archive. 121 Range/Bettmann,
TR, B. 122 Range/Bettmann, TL, B;
Robert Opie Collection, MM. 123
Patrimonie Photographie/Photograph
by Andre Kertész. 124 Range/
Bettmann. 125 Science Picture
Library, TL, TR; Range/Bettmann
Archive, BR. 126 Ullstein
Bilderdienst. 127 G.L.C. Library, TL,
TR; Robert Opie Collection, B. 128
Ullstein Bilderdienst, TL; M.E.P.L.,
TR. 129 Royal Flying Doctor Service,
Queensland,TR; M.E.P.L., B. 130
Robert Opie Collection, T; Hulton-
Deutsch, B. 131 University of
Louisville, T; M.E.P.L., B. 132
Range/Bettmann, T; Topham Picture
Source, B. 133 Range/Bettmann. 134
Hulton-Deutsch. 135 Ullstein
Bilderdienst, T; Robert Opie
Collection, BL, BM, BR. 136 Ullstein
Bilderdienst. 137 Library of
Congress. 138 Arthur Lockwood, TL,
TR; Hulton-Deutsch, B. 139 Hulton-
Deutsch, TL; Range/Bettmann, BL,
BR. 140, 141 Range/Bettmann. 142
Robert Opie Collection, T; Range/
Bettmann, B. 143 Brown Brothers, T;
Range/Bettmann, MR. 144 Range/
Bettmann, TL, TR. 145 Robert Opie
Collection, TR, BM. 146 Range/
Bettmann. 147 T.B.A., TL, BR;
Range/Bettmann, TR, BL. 148
Range/Bettmann, TL, TR. 149
Range/Bettmann. 150 Range/
Bettmann/UPI, TL, TR, ML, MR, BL,
BR; Hulton-Deutsch, MM. 151
Hulton-Deutsch, TL, BR; Popperfoto,
TR; Roger-Viollet, MM; The Reader's
Digest Association Limited, BL. 152
Hulton-Deutsch, TL,TR, MM;
Range/Bettmann/UPI, MR, BL, BR.
153 Arthur Lockwood, TL; Range/
Bettmann, TR; Popperfoto, ML;
Hulton-Deutsch, MM, BL, BR;
Ullstein Bilderdienst, MR. 154
Hulton-Deutsch, T, MM; Courtesy
Penguin Books Limited, ML;
Range/Bettmann, MR; M.E.P.L., B.
155 Hulton-Deutsch, TL, TR;
Popperfoto, ML, MM, MR; Camera
Press, B.

The publishers are grateful to the
following individuals and
publishers for their kind
permission to quote passages from
the publications below:

Allen Lane, The Penguin Press from
Akenfield by Ronald Blyth, 1969.
A.P. Watt on behalf of The Trustees
of the Robert Graves Copyright Trust
from *The Long Weekend* by Robert
Graves.
Batsford Ltd from *A History of
Everyday Things in England* by

Marjorie and C.H.B. Quennell, 1986.
BBC Books from *Australia: Beyond
the Dreamtime* by Thomas Keneally,
Patsy Adam-Smith and Robyn
Davidson.
The Literary Trustees of the late Sir
Cecil Beaton from Cecil Beaton
writing in *Vogue* Magazine, 1920s.
Chatto & Windus from *Cider With
Rosie* by Laurie Lee, 1959.
Solo from *Daily Mail*.
Executors of the Estate of the late
Emlyn Williams from *George* by
Emlyn Williams.
Express Newspapers from *Daily
Express*, 1935.
Harold Ober Associates from *This
Side Of Paradise* by Scott Fitzgerald,
Bodley Head.
HarperCollins Publishers from *Only
Yesterdays* by Frederick Allen,
Harper & Row, 1931.
John Murray Ltd from *Pillar To Post,
The Pocket Lamp of Architecture* by
Osbert Lancaster, 1938.
Penguin Books from *The Pelican
Social History of Britain: British
Society, 1914-45* by John Stevenson,
© John Stevenson, 1984.
Peters Fraser & Dunlop Group Ltd
from *The Glory And The Dream* by
William Manchester.
Random House UK from *Tuppence
To Cross The Mersey* by Helen
Forrester, Bodley Head, and *Nairn in
Darkness & Light* by David
Thomson, Hutchinson.
Robin Clark Ltd from *The Green Hat*
by Michael Arlen, 1991.
Routledge from *Plenty And Want* by
John Burnett, 1930s.
Scribner, an Imprint of Simon &
Schuster, Inc., from *By-Line* by
Ernest Hemingway, edited by
W.White. Copyright © 1967 by Mary
Hemingway. Scribner Library
Edition from German Inflation, (pp.
46-47), originally published in
Toronto Star, September 19, 1922.
Estate of the late Sonia Brownell
Orwell and Secker & Warburg Ltd
from *England Your England and
Other Essays* and *Keep the Aspidistra
Flying*.
Victor Gollancz from *The Citadel* by
A.J. Cronin.
Copyright 1939 Renewed © 1967 by
John Steinbeck Reprinted by
Permission of William Heinemann
Ltd and Viking Penguin from *The
Grapes Of Wrath* by John Steinbeck,
1939.

Front cover: Range/Bettmann, TL;
Library of Congress, MM; Robert
Opie Collection, MR, BL, BM; Hulton-
Deutsch, BR.

Back cover: Range/Bettmann,TL,
MR; Robert Opie Collection, TM, ML,
BR; M.E.P.L., TR.